Natural Language

A Clinician-Guided Program for Parents of Language-Delayed Children

by
John T. Hatten, Ph.D.
and
Pequetti W. Hatten, M.S.

REVISED EDITION
1981

A word about "he" and "she" and "him" and "her."

Although we are in complete philosophical agreement with recent attempts to make our language less sex biased, we have yet to find such a language form which is not so awkward as to make it offensive in itself. For this reason, we have tried to use pronoun forms that appear to best fit the context, and we intend absolutely no bias or discrimination in their use.

About the Authors

JOHN HATTEN received his Ph.D. from the University of Wisconsin in 1965, where he completed his dissertation on the topic of clinical supervision. Since that time he has taught at Northern Michigan University and the University of Minnesota, Duluth, where he is currently Professor in the Department of Communicative Disorders and director of the graduate program.

As a former public school speech clinician, Dr. Hatten's primary interests are language disorders in children and clinical speech services in the schools. His recent publications include *Diagnosis and Evaluation in Speech Pathology* by L. Emerick and John Hatten (Prentice-Hall, 1979), and *Emerging Language* by John Hatten, Tracy Goman and Carole Lent (Communication Skill Builders, Inc., 1981).

PEQUETTI HATTEN received her M.S. degree from Purdue University in 1961. She has worked professionally as a speech clinician in Downer's Grove, Illinois, and Madison, Wisconsin, and taught in the Department of Speech at Northern Michigan University. She is currently a speech clinician in the Duluth Public Schools. Mrs. Hatten co-authored an article with her husband relating their experiences with a nonverbal foster child (*Journal of Speech and Hearing Disorders,* volume 36, no. 2, 1971). She uses her experiences as a mother and speech clinician to develop practical ideas for parents that can be incorporated into the routine of day-to-day living.

The Hattens have two daughters and enjoy tennis, gardening, fishing, and the outdoor beauty of northern Minnesota.

Contents

To the Parents

We do not expect you to become a language teacher; nor do we intend to tell you to stop doing what you have been doing with your child.

Rather, we want you to relate to your child in the natural environment of your home, and to keep an affectionate, warm, and spontaneous attitude. Maintain all the daily tasks and interactions of your family, for it is the home setting and the daily interactions that are the keys to language development. You have what no language clinician has — contact with your child for the major portion of his waking hours, and many daily, real–life situations requiring the use of language.

As you select and use sections of this booklet and as you work with the clinician who supplied it to you, we hope these ideas for improving language skills will encourage you to seek other language–learning situations on your own. Keep in contact with the clinician, ask questions, and report areas of difficulty and progress. It may not be easy at first. It may require planning and forethought where none was required before, thinking before you speak, or modifying daily routine. Remember, the easy and spontaneous home environment is a gold mine of opportunity — because you are the most important influence on your child's language behavior.

People tend to learn best about those things that are most important to them at the moment. If you are currently working on your tax returns, you know how interested you are in conversations about that process. On the other hand, you probably listen only passively to topics that are not related to your current concerns; for example, discussions about food just do not interest us directly after a big meal. The following pages contain suggestions for language stimulation. However, if the activities, topics, or materials are not of interest to your child, you would be well advised to change them to be more appealing.

At the same time, if your child has some current issue in his life that is preoccupying his attention (for example, illness, the upcoming move of a friend, or a lost dog), you probably should attend to that issue prior to working on the specific activities we present. Remember, those issues in themselves may become excellent language teaching experiences.

Of course, this same precaution applies to you as a parent. If you have some pressing personal problem that makes effective interaction with your child difficult, try to solve the problem first. We agree that this advice is easier said than done, but in general, the *quality* of your interaction with your child is just as important as the *quantity* of interaction.

Your potential for helping cannot be overemphasized! Recently, a parent of one of the children we were working with said, "*You* teach him to talk; he just won't do a thing for me!" It took a good deal of talking to convince that mother that she was a very important part of the process. In many areas of early childhood education, research has shown that programs that do not include *active parent participation* have very little long-term effect. On the other hand, programs that involve the parents to a high degree not only show improved results, but the positive changes are more lasting. You are not just an important part of this process; you are *the* most important part.

To the Clinician

This book is intended as a clinician-guided program for parents. It is expected that the clinician will be involved and stay involved in an ongoing parent program. The clinician and parent will decide which sections are appropriate for a particular child, and which sections or parts of a section will be the responsibility of the parent and which the responsibility of the clinician. Translated into language for IEP writing, this might mean a Level II (indirect), with parent or surrogate parent providing service by carrying out both natural and structured goals; a Level II, with parent carrying out only naturalistic goals; and a Level III, with the clinician providing structured goals and the parent providing natural goals as a follow-up.

Clinician Responsibilities:

1. Know the child's needs. (This is not the scope of this book, but it is too important not to state at the beginning.)

2. Know the parents. How much do they wish or are they able to be involved?

3. Introduce this book to the parents and discuss the general concepts that apply specifically to the child in question. If you want to modify some parts for your own purposes, now is the time to do so.

4. Along with the parents, decide who will be responsible for sections or subsections; write this information on the IEP if one is being written for this child. If possible, demonstrate for the parent how to carry out a few sections.

5. Use the activity checklist in Appendix A to assign sections, and let the parents mark them off as they are completed (see page 89).

6. Set a time for completion of the assigned section and a date for follow–up meeting.

7. Meet with the parents and review the section completed. Check to see that the procedures are working. Check to see that the parents understand and are comfortable with the program. If possible, try to observe what they are doing. Answer any questions they may have.

8. Suggest another section and begin the process again.

Introduction

The best way to teach your child how to speak is not to teach him at all.

The word *teaching* sounds too much like structured lessons and formal instruction. Speech is best learned under the natural conditions of playing and growing up. Although the suggestions in this book call for some "teaching" on the part of the parent, it is always best to maintain a natural and spontaneous nature when dealing with your child. *Language is learned, but it is not taught.* Always try to make the activities fun, easy, and natural. That is the right environment for language growth.

Parents play a unique role in their child's speech and language development. A pre–school child spends the majority of his day with his parents. His world revolves around his family. A parent's world, on the other hand, is wider in scope and filled with demands and responsibilities outside of the home. This situation brings about a perplexing discrepancy in outlook. Whereas the parents are the totality of the child's world, the child is only a part (although admittedly a very important part) of the parent's world.

We have written this book with this in mind, and we hope that as you read it you will not experience feelings of frustration and burden. Our ideas are offered as suggestions to prod your imagination and to give some structure to what you do in the language–development area. We intend for this to be a fun venture between parent and child. We are fully aware that the best parents in the world have never read any books on how to be a good parent, and the best interaction between parent and child is the natural interaction that comes out of love and trust and the sheer joy of being together.

When a child fails to learn to talk within a reasonable length of time (say, the first two–and–one–half years of life), it sometimes becomes necessary to adjust the amount of time and energy devoted to that child. We believe that this book is uniquely designed to lessen the possibility of undue hardship, since the suggestions are designed to help you help your child learn language

while making maximum use of the *normal routine of family life.*
Our theme cannot be stressed too often: children normally do
not learn the complicated rules of language and the complex
processes of speech in formal teacher–student lessons. They learn
language best in the usual give-and-take of everyday life. This
should be good news to most parents, since it means that much
of what you are already doing provides superb language stimulation. Reading this book will no doubt prove to you that you
are already a very effective "language teacher." We hope it will
give you a few ideas on how to become even more effective.

This book provides suggestions for parents relating to three
areas of child development: language–related skills, pre–language
sensory skills, and language skills. These categories are a bit arbi-
trary, and no child learns in neat little parcels, but a breakdown
of skills is helpful in organization. First, the section entitled
Language-Related Skills discusses the topics of behavior, self-
awareness, and muscle coordination. Second, by the term *pre-
language sensory skills,* we mean the various forms of learning
that are dependent upon the senses of seeing, hearing, and feeling. And last, the *language skills* section, of course, deals with
the actual task of learning how to talk using the system of rules
we call language. *Language* is a system of rules that we use to
learn sentence forms, word meanings, and so forth. *Speech,*
however, is talking (i.e., using that language system to communicate by using sounds produced by control of our breathing,
voice box, and mouth).

Each section of the book is parceled into separate units providing ideas for both daily–life situations and more structured
"sit–down" activities. The suggestions and activities in the units
are intended as springboards to stimulate ideas suited to your
particular child. An attempt has been made to present a cross-
section of many areas and activities of a family's daily home
and community environment and to relate these settings to language development experiences. The activities mentioned are
presented only as examples, and they are interchangeable from
one area to another. You may find ways to adapt them for use
in several skill areas, and you will certainly find many ways to
modify the activities to suit your home and lifestyle.

THE TARGET OF THIS BOOK

Our efforts are for parents of the child who:

1. does not appear to understand when others speak to him, even though it is evident that he hears adequately.

2. has a small speaking vocabulary for his age.

3. appears to be having difficulty learning how to link words together to make sentences.

4. is having difficulty knowing which words to choose in performing such language functions as making a word plural, changing tense, indicating possession, using pronouns, etc.

5. is not only using a limited vocabulary but whose speech contains many sound–making errors. In addition, it is difficult or impossible to understand him.

6. is unable to perform the following tasks: name common objects, tell what common objects are used for, make requests, give directions, indicate possession of objects, relate a recent experience, ask questions, answer questions, engage in fantasy and yet know the difference between fantasy and reality, indicate where things are by location, say "no" or indicate negation, etc. (Since language is such an all–important human function, this list could go on and on. We have stopped here in the hope that the reader has a general flavor of what we are looking for.)

DANGER SIGNALS

Keep in mind that a good deal of variation is normal. However, the following behaviors should tell you to look further into the problem if:

- by four months, the child does not smile or respond to familiar faces.
- by six months, the child does not respond differently to different speech inflections (for example, angry vs. friendly).
- by eight months, the child is not babbling.
- by twelve months, the child does not understand any words.
- by eighteen months, the child does not speak any words.
- by twenty–four months, the child does not understand and point appropriately when asked to show his mouth.
- by twenty–seven months, the child is not using any two-word combinations.

- by thirty–six months, the child is not easily understood most of the time.

- by thirty–six months, the child is not using short sentences to communicate.

- by forty–eight months, the child is not totally intelligible in conversational speech.

- by forty–eight months, the child does not speak sentences that sound almost adult–like.

At the end of this book is a checklist to help you take an organized look at your child's communication skills (see Appendix B, page 93).

In other words, this book is for those parents whose children are having greater than usual difficulty learning to speak. Since no single child will need to go through every step of this book, and since certain portions will be more helpful for your child than others, *we urge you to keep in close contact with the speech clinician or other trained professional who provided this book for you.*

This book is to be used by parents in conjunction with on-going speech and language work conducted by a speech clinician or with the guidance from a speech clinician and ongoing evaluation by both. Although these techniques and suggestions have proven helpful to many children, remember that not all children learn in the same manner. If you have given honest effort and your child is not making continued and promising progress toward adequate speech and language, a change in procedure may be appropriate.

SOME GENERAL SUGGESTIONS

1. *Try to attach a pleasurable feeling to speech.* For many children, attempting to communicate has become associated with failure. Attempting to speak has become punishing and unpleasant — too many attempts have met with reprimand.

2. *Reward your child's attempts to speak.* Smile and respond warmly even if you do not understand every word. Try to let the child know you are happy that he is trying to talk. Don't expect adult standards from your child.

3. *Gesture communication is often a problem* for parents of children who don't speak. Parents often believe that their child has learned to gesture rather than learning to talk.

Rarely is this the case, however. Gesturing is an important part of normal language development. If you feel that your child is gesturing *rather* than talking, it is best to speak the words that reflect the child's gestured desires. In this way you are giving the child a model of the type of communication you are expecting from him. Remember to keep your language simple, slow, and short.

4. *Reward speech attempts, but don't punish the lack of them.* Children learn to speak when the environment is one of acceptance and approving relationships. If a word attempt is poorly spoken or inaccurate, don't say "No . . . it isn't oop, it's soup." Rather, show your approval for the attempt and repeat the word correctly. Children learn to speak by comparing their words with yours. Once you tell your child that he is *wrong,* he may hear nothing else and soon come to think that speaking is difficult and something he doesn't do well.

5. *Set up conditions to help language development when your child is ready* rather than push him when he isn't ready.

SPECIAL RECOMMENDATIONS

1. Don't speak too rapidly. Many children who have trouble learning language can't understand rapid speech. Slow down! Speak at a slower than usual rate.

2. Speak in short statements with simple but correct grammar.

3. Don't interrupt your child's speech attempts. Sometimes this is difficult, but set some rules so that he doesn't feel that he must hurry what he is saying before someone else takes the floor.

4. Give your child your full attention whenever possible. The "token" listener is one who gives only casual attention to the speaker. Be sure your child knows that what he says is of importance to you.

5. Speak to your child. Verbal stimulation is of great importance, even if your child does not speak himself.

6. Have your child watch and listen. When you are talking to him, try to be, physically, at his eye level.

7. When engaging in speech stimulation activities, choose a time when your child is well rested and attentive. Don't pursue an activity to the point of boredom.

8. Know what is normal for your child. Don't accept less, and don't demand what is unrealistic.

9. Carefully selected toys can aid language development. Construction materials and toys that have a variety of textures, shapes, and colors are helpful. Every child is different in the way he learns. Some children seem to be interested in *people* and react to the moods, ideas, requests, and so on, that people present. Other children learn more about *things* in their world. These children are more interested in how things work, how they go together, and so on, and they may spend more time with toys and playthings than with people. Both these ways of learning about the world work, but you may wish to study your child to see if there is a definite pattern. Knowing your child's pattern may help you in the selection of toys and other language stimulation materials. Although it would be impossible to suggest appropriate toys for all age groups, some general ideas about the best toys for language stimulation might help. Select toys that:

   a. you can do things with (such as roll, stack, connect, slide, etc.).

   b. change shape, color, or sound (such as clay, music makers, etc.).

   c. can be used to pretend about real life experiences (such as play phones, toy dishes, miniature cars, etc.).

   d. help the child learn to put things in categories (such as circle, square, and triangle games; matching; sorting; etc.).

   e. have real working parts rather than solid or stationary parts.

   f. have high interest value because of their particularly unique color, shape, size, smell, or texture.

10. Don't talk about you child's speech or language problems in front of him. Remember, you want him to enjoy speaking. If other adults bring up the topic, be sure you convey your confidence in your child. "We're working on it, and he's doing fine," should do the trick.

11. If your child begins hesitating in speech attempts, repeating phrases or words, or prolonging sounds, don't assume that he is beginning to stutter. "Mommy, mommy, mommy, I want, I want, I want, I want, I want to go, go, go outside," may represent perfectly normal speech for a three-, four-

or five-year-old child. Such behavior in young children is quite normal. If you take time to listen to your own speech, you will notice that you are not fluent 100 percent of the time, either. Notice when your child is having difficulty — particularly when he's tired or excited. It would be wise not to make speech demands of him at these times. Make speech a pleasant event, something he enjoys very much. If you are concerned about his speech, remember that this concern will be easily communicated to your child. The best policy is to regard the hesitations and repetitions as normal, neither being unduly interested in them nor overly ignoring them.

12. Avoid undue pressure. Don't try too many things at a time. Language development is a long, slow process at best, and when it involves some special problems, much work may be involved. Set flexible timetables for yourself or your child. Parents often get upset and frustrated with their children, and this is of no help to anyone.

13. If you cannot understand your child's speech attempts, remember that it is frustrating for *both* of you. When he says "I a ahah," he thinks he is speaking just as clearly as when you say "I want water." You might try acknowledging his frustration. "It's hard to say that." Express your own shortcomings by saying something like "Mom can't always say things when she wants to, either." In another part of your day, show him that you have trouble saying things, too. His speech patterns are not indications of laziness but rather of entrenched habits or underdeveloped skills. As your child progresses, you may sometimes understand only one word from an utterance. Try to acknowledge that word by repeating it, using a sentence like "Tell me more about _____ ."

14. Parents often have difficulty in responding to the grammar or naming the errors that their children make. We have found it most helpful to respond in ways that encourage the child to search further for the correct word. Some examples of this are as follows:

   a. If your child looks at a cup and says "glass," you could respond by saying "No, it's a cup." However, in doing so you would have ended the child's search for the correct word. A better alternative might be to say "We drink out of glasses. What else do we drink from?" "What does Dad put his coffee in?" "Is it a glass or a cup?"

b. If you ask your child to bring you a pillow and he returns with a blanket, try saying "The blanket will keep me warm, but a pillow will be soft under my head." Such a response should help him correct his error.

15. Take every opportunity to enjoy your child as he is.

PART I:

Language-Related Skills

This section is devoted to three topics related to language development. The first deals with *behavioral characteristics* of children with language problems and offers some general suggestions and tentative answers to the most common questions. The second topic provides suggestions for working on *self-awareness.* Some researchers believe that a child's image of himself as a person is directly related to his speech and language development. The third topic deals with *coordination* and offers some activities aimed at assisting development of general motor skill.

Each of these is only introductory in nature. If your child has particular difficulty with behavioral control, self-concept, and/or muscle coordination, we suggest that you seek further professional assistance.

Although behavior that is generally disruptive need not necessarily interfere with a child's language learning, there are times when this is the case. The following are circumstances in which the child's behavior may become a factor in his failure to learn the language system.

1. *The child is not interacting with his family.*

By a very early age, most children have begun to smile and show social awareness. Such responsiveness is a crucial element in language-learning, since the model of the language to be learned is going to be provided by the people near the child. If your child appears to be simply oblivious to what is happening around him, this is an important danger signal and should prompt you to seek professional assistance. Too often, parents and physicians are beguiled by the thought that the child will outgrow his problems, only to find that prevention would have been significantly easier and more productive than later remedial work. Community mental hygiene centers or human development centers are an excellent source of assistance for such children, and they can provide meaningful help for the family as well as the child. Many parents find that once they have the feeling that something constructive is being done, much of the emotional tension related to the child's behavior disappears and family interaction improves.

2. The child is overactive and easily distracted.

"Hyperactive" is an overused and much–misunderstood word. All of us are hyperactive and easily distracted at one time or another, and children are no exception. Certain children stand out, however, as being almost driven to motor and mental activity levels beyond all reason. Such children move purposelessly from one object or activity to another without end.

Two points appear to be most important in judging whether your child's activity level is unnaturally high. First, do his activities appear to have little or no real goal in mind? Does he move about without really going anywhere? Banging his head, rocking, swaying from foot to foot, and biting himself or others are all typical of hyperactive children and should be of concern.

The second major danger signal concerns the general level of activity in relation to age and environment. There may well be no such thing as hyperactivity in three–year–olds; they are just naturally so active that the concept of being overactive is meaningless. But if your child stands out in a group of children his own age as being far more active, aggressive, and distractible than the others, we suggest that you take note.

3. The child does not need language.

There are children who appear to have found alternate methods for getting things done. Although language is a crucial and natural part of human behavior, it appears that some children are capable of doing without it. Parents often say the older brothers and sisters do everything for the child, or that he is simply satisfied getting his needs met through grunts and gestures. But clearly there is more to it than that.

If you feel that your child is not learning to talk because he simply doesn't need to, you should do two things. First, set out purposefully to look for other reasons. Few, if any, children don't talk because they lack the motivation. Second, make sure that your child has every reason to enjoy talking and finds it to be a rewarding experience.

Use firm but understanding methods and attempt to eliminate those times during the day when your child can get his reward without speech. If he grunts or points his finger to get a drink of water, demand a bit more. Do not, of course, demand a complete sentence or even a clearly stated "water," but try to elicit something that resembles an attempt at the word. If you respond to the request and tell him why he got the water ("You did a good job of asking.''), this will enhance the effectiveness. Remember that there is potential for frustration here, so try to move at a pace your child can tolerate.

4. The child is generally well behaved but has begun to echo much of what others say.

Echolaila, a fancy word for the child's repeating of what others have said, is a common characteristic of some language-delayed children. It is sometimes called "parroting."

For example, some children respond to "Do you want a drink of water?" with "Drink of water." Although some of the language is meaningful and to the point, a great deal is not. If the behavior continues to a significant degree beyond the third year, professional help from a speech and language clinician is recommended.

We have found that many of the patterned questions we ask children almost encourage echoing, so we have set out to encourage parents to attempt to eliminate them. Social greetings such as "Hi! How are you?" and "What is your name?" are frequently triggers that bring about the echo response. Parents of echoing children are often asked to look carefully at how they phrase things. "More bread, Jimmy?" is more likely to receive a meaningful response from the child.

Similarly, it is recommended that parents do not reinforce the echoed statement by laughing, giving the child what he wants, or generally responding in a positive manner. The best response is probably none at all, with a rephrased statement following in a few seconds.

Getting your child to pay attention to the important elements of the various stimuli around him is a key to language-learning. You may find some of the following suggestions useful:

- Such children often thrive on routine and structure. We are certainly not encouraging compulsive daily rituals, but we do encourage a pattern that gives the child a feeling of comfort and predictability.

- You may find it to your child's benefit to avoid situations in which a great deal of noise, confusion, and random activity are present. Parties attended by many children, unsupervised playgrounds, and so on, may simply provide too much stimulation and should be avoided to some degree.

• Try to control the amount of toys your child has so that he is not continuously overwhelmed with mountains of playthings spread over the floor. Some parents find it productive to rotate the toy stock so that only a certain amount is available at one time. A good rule of thumb: there should only be as many toys available as there are storage containers for them.

• Prepare your child for upcoming changes. For example, if you are taking a trip, be sure he is well informed. It is a good idea to talk about the trip a few days in advance and to talk about what you will be doing and how you will get from place to place. It would be helpful to show him pictures of the places to be visited.

• If it is possible to comfortably slow down the pace of your life, this may be of real help. One mother we recently worked with gave up her volunteer work at a local hospital when she realized that this added trip out each week was only adding to her own tension and nervousness.

The remaining sections of this book follow this format: (a) a brief explanation of the skill area to be developed, (b) specific activities to incorporate into the natural home environment, and (c) more structured activities devised to develop the skill area.

SELF–AWARENESS

Help your child understand who he is and what he is. Self-awareness is the ability to relate to surroundings and the ability to communicate this relationship.

Body Image

Natural

a. A full–length mirror would be useful for this activity. If you do not have one, hang a large mirror at your child's level and in a convenient place that you both frequently pass during the day. As you pass the mirror, begin an "I-See" activity. "I see you (or Johnny) in the mirror. I see me (or Mommy) in the mirror. I see your head in the mirror . . . your arm, leg, etc." Then ask him to point in the mirror to his head, arm, leg, etc., and your head, arm, leg, etc. It may be necessary to stay with one part of the body for one day or a few days and then gradually add the others. Children sometimes enjoy finding their eyes, hair, nose, etc., when looking at the side of a shiny pot or pan or chrome strip, especially when their features appear larger or smaller than normal. Occasions such as these frequently arise in the kitchen. Try to make use of these opportunities. Setting a mirror in front of the child while he eats a meal will sometimes aid in calling attention to facial parts.

b. An outdoor activity to help your child identify body parts is "Angels in the Snow." The child lies down in relatively fresh snow, arms and legs out, then gets up carefully to see his image in the show. Again ask him to point to parts of his body. This activity can also be done at the beach in smooth sand.

c. In the bathtub, ask your child to identify head, ears, neck, arms, etc., as he is washed, rinsed, and dried. Make it fun; put a word or phrase with it, if you wish, which is repeated with each part, such as "Scrub, scrub head; splash, splash arm; pat, pat leg." etc.

Structured

a. Using a large piece of paper, taped-together newspapers, or a large flattened cardboard box, draw the outline of your child's body while he is lying down, arms and legs away from his body. Give attention to fingers and distinctive features, such as long or short hair or a pony-tail. Together fill in and color the features and details (mouth, eyes, hair, fingernails, clothing, etc.) and cut around the figure. Have your child point to and repeat (if he wishes) the parts of his body ("This is my arm, head, etc."). Accept whatever response he gives — a word, a pointed finger, etc.

b. Take a photograph (full length) of your child. Ask him to describe himself. "What color are your eyes? How tall are you?" Pointing may be his only response at first. Ask him to compare his own characteristics and features with those of other people, of animals, or objects. "How many legs do you have? How many legs does the dog have? How many legs does the chair have?" Show him pictures of animals, other members of his family, his friends, etc., to help him make comparisons.

c. Tear out a picture of a child or some animals from a coloring book and cut it up simply into parts: head, trunk, arms, legs. Have your child put the parts back together with glue, and color them. Encourage him to name the parts as he works and to verbalize what he is doing. It may be necessary for you to verbalize it for him, but be sensitive to his attempts.

d. Take dolls or stuffed animals and point out the head, arms, legs, body. Make a game with a small blanket or piece of material. Cover a part of the doll and name the part that is covered or ask him to do it: "Put the bear's leg to sleep."

e. Make a body out of "Play–Doh." This can sometimes be a difficult task for a young child, and he may need help and encouragement. "Our man needs a leg. Let's make him a leg. Now he needs another leg. He can walk with his legs. What else can he do with his legs? He has very short, fat legs," etc. Use the same ideas when putting the dough away. "Oops, there goes the man's head in the box. His arm wants to go, too. The other arm is going to chase it. Now he's all gone."

f. The "Cootie" or "Mr. Potato Head" games give your child an opportunity to put objects together, part by part. The children's record of "Hokey Pokey" teaches body awareness in an entertaining fashion.

Self–Concept

Help your child understand how he feels about himself. This is an ongoing process – something to be incorporated into daily interaction.

Natural

a. Point out the things he does well. "Yes, you can put on your coat all by yourself."

b. Agree to the difficulty of the task. "Learning to put on your coat is hard to do. Getting that arm in the right place is hard work."

c. Point out how he has improved. "When you were two years old, you didn't know how to put on your coat. Now you can do it yourself."

d. Express confidence that he will be able to do more in the future. "I'm sure you will learn to button your coat sometime soon." In the meantime, find many opportunities during the day to point out to him the things he *can* do.

e. Several times each day, make a conscious effort to describe and discuss your emotions. Children often see (and feel) the end result of parental emotions but seldom hear parents objectively describe how they feel.

f. Allow your child to express *his* emotions and be sure to show your understanding. A stubbed toe or pinched finger may elicit from you a consoling "It will be OK soon." However, it may be more helpful for your child to indicate your understanding. "I can see how that would hurt. My finger hurts when I pinch it, too." Be sure you do the same thing when the hurt is psychological. "I can see why you're angry. Jimmy broke your toy car, and you liked that car very much."

Structured

a. Look through magazines or books and find pictures of people displaying various emotions — sadness, happiness, anger, contentment, etc. Talk about how they feel. Relate these to times when your child is sad, happy, etc. Stress the point that everyone has these feelings at times. Verbalize to your child the times when you are sad or happy. "I can't get the car to start and that makes me feel angry inside."

b. Using hand puppets, play the "I'll Bet He's _____" game. Take a puppet and carry on a "pretend" conversation using nonsense words and various voices (loud for angry, soft for sad, etc.). Have various family members attempt to guess at the emotion being displayed.

c. A set of family puppets will be helpful in many language activities described later in this book, but for now they could be used in play fashion to emphasize various family relationships — father, mother, sister, etc.

MOTOR SKILL AND COORDINATION

Balance

A child's ability to steady himself or be in a state of equilibrium varies with age. The child learns to sit alone, sit and reach, stand while holding, stand alone, walk, run, etc., in his mastery of the skill of balancing. Balance is important to language in that it is a maturational step along the way. Children with language difficulties should be provided with opportunities to develop their balancing skills to a reasonable degree.

Natural

a. Have your child practice putting one foot in front of the other by walking forward, backward, or sideways. Have him walk the edge of a sidewalk or a crack in the sidewalk. Encourage him by saying things like "Okay, you're the tightrope walker in the circus. Stay on the line. Oh, it's a long way down. Better not look. Keep your head up," etc. A more realistic "tightrope" might be the edge of the sandbox or the top of a low concrete wall. The same activity can be carried on inside the home by using a pattern in the rug or flooring that your child "tightrope walks" each time he passes that particular area.

Structured

a. Place a rope or piece of yarn on the floor in a straight line or in various shapes, winding it in patterns without touching another part of the rope. You can say "Let's walk the path to Grandmother's house. I hope we don't meet the big, bad wolf." You may use colored papers as the path. If your child takes a particular fancy to the story of *The Wizard of Oz,* it is fun to play "Follow the Yellow Brick Road" with this activity. It also can be played with a two–by–four board turned on either side. You should encourage him to keep his head up by designating an object or picture to watch while he walks, or by taping a colored square on the wall for him. "We have to keep watching for the wicked witch." Make the task more difficult by putting something in his hand to carry – "Better carry the oil can for the tin man."

b. Make a game of one–leg stand. Time your child to see how long he can stand on the right leg, then the left; then repeat the same activity while he holds something in his hand.

c. Play "Balance Battle." You and your child each hold one end of a rope and stand on a cut–out paper "ship." Play tug-o'-war to see who can pull the other off the ship.

Locomotion

Moving oneself from one place to another can be accomplished by walking, running, hopping, skipping, jumping, sliding, crawling, etc. Although there is no direct link between walking and the development of speech and language development, locomotion skills are a part of the total maturation of the child.

Natural

a. Many outdoor activities can be adapted to this skill area. You can walk, run, skip, etc., at different times during a trip to the store, to see a neighbor, or at any outing.

b. Utilize outdoor play materials also. Adding a tire or a tunnel to back yard play equipment affords opportunities to show the child things like "That tire is really tough. We can walk on it, jump on it, hop in and out of it, crawl through it, etc. We can do it fast or slow. What else can we do with the tire?"

c. Suggest that your child crawl along with you while you dust the furniture. Let him crawl through and around chairs, tables, etc., and help by dusting the bottom legs at the same time. Be sure to verbalize to him what he is doing.

d. Exercise for the family pet is another area easily adapted to locomotion skills. "Walk the dog, or hop, or jump the dog," usually sounds strange enough to be intriguing to a small child.

Structured

a. Using bright tape, designate areas or dots or short strips in a kitchen, hallway, or recreation room floor for walking, running, skipping, or hopping activities. Have your child walk on the strips, walk in between them, hop on them, hop in between them, etc. "We are crossing the river on these rocks; stay on, or you will get your feet wet." Play the "Trip to Grandmother's House" or "Follow the Yellow Brick Road," as suggested under balance activities, above, in the same manner.

b. Many children enjoy these activities when the various skills are given animal names. "Let's be an elephant (walk slowly), horse or other favorite animal (walk fast), kangaroo (big hops), a grasshopper (little hops), turtle (slow crawl)."

c. Play "Treasure Hunt" and hide a prize, toy, or candy in a certain place and give your child directions to find it. "Walk to the dining room, crawl under the table, hop to the green chair," etc. Do it with him; then see if he can do it with verbal directions only.

d. "Musical Chairs" is another traditional party game easily adapted to improve locomotion skills.

e. "I'm Going on a Lion Hunt" is another traditional game where the child acts out walking through the forest, climbing mountains, crawling through tall grass, crossing the muddy river, etc., and then returns home in the reverse order.

Rhythm

A good place to start with rhythm is to build an awareness in your child of when sound is present and when it is not. Ask him to respond in some bodily way when an agreed–upon sound is present (such as clapping hands, marching feet, tapping fingers or pencils, beating drum, etc.), and to stop the activity when the sound is not present. Later this can be expanded into more complicated rhythms.

Natural

a. Heighten your child's awareness to rhythm. Hold him on your lap, arms around him, while you rock in a chair, first slowly, then faster, or in a different rhythm. You can incorporate sounds with the movement of the chair. "Our rocking chair is old and tired. When it moves, it groans – mmm . . . mmm . . . mmm . . . mmm. Now our rocking chair is a boy (or a girl) who wants to go fast – eee . . . eee . . . eee . . . eee."

b. Rhythm is a part of many household appliances, such as a clock, dishwasher, washing machine, dryer, etc. Make your child aware of these rhythms. "Listen, the washing machine is singing us a song." Make a bodily movement (moving arms from side to side, for instance). Try to verbalize with the rhythm. "See, I can be a washing machine. Wish, wash, wish, wash. You try it."

Structured

a. "Musical Chairs" is a game that has been teaching children to be aware of the presence and absence of sound for many years. Use a record player or noisemaker, child's toy, etc., and direct your child, "March when you hear the music. Find a chair and sit in it when the music stops."

b. Play a hand–clapping imitation game. Sometimes being allowed to wear mother's or dad's gloves helps to add a bit of interest to this game. Clap . . . clap . . . clap, clap, clap . . clap. Ask him to imitate you. "We are clowns in the circus, and we are trying to get all of the people to clap with us." Try this activity in front of a large mirror.

c. There are many good children's records and commercial records with marching rhythms. Use these and clap hands, march, beat drums, or use other bodily activities in rhythm with the music. Do not be discouraged if your child is not immediately able to imitate various rhythms or keep in time to music. This is a difficult task for many children, and people vary greatly in their inherent "time–keeping" abilities. When holding your child, try to get a sense of your child's body rhythm. Everyone seems to have a rhythm basic to their physical–emotional makeup. Try to point these rhythms out to your child, and try to imitate them yourself.

Eye–Hand Coordination

Eye–hand coordination is a term referring to the ability to direct the movements of the hand by seeing where the hands are going and what they are doing.

Natural

a. Make a point of watching your child while he is playing with his toys. Are the toys too small and intricate? Do they encourage frustration and failure? Be sure his toys are large enough so that he can manipulate them with ease and confidence.

b. Encouraging self–help on your child's part may mean a few spilled glasses of milk, but it also can promote self–confidence. Allow your child to do some of the routine things that call for a certain amount of eye–hand coordination. For example, let him pour milk on his cereal, drizzle honey on toast, dress and undress himself, tie his shoes, dry dishes, etc.

Structured

a. Coloring, painting, and drawing can promote good hand control. With young children, start with color crayons and newspapers. Good old–fashioned scribbling will result, but that is certainly to be preferred to a coloring book or other restricting picture.

b. Games that call for accuracy are helpful in developing eye–hand skill. The new lightweight, sponge rubber balls are great for games of basketball (using a wastebasket) or bowling (using a few empty milk cartons).

c. Paper–and–pencil games that call for accuracy are also good. Start with very simple tasks, such as having the child draw a line between two points on a paper (one point could be home and the other school). The child's task is to bring the boy from home to school. Later, tasks can be made more complicated. You might eventually include simple mazes and tracing pictures.

PART II

Pre-Language Sensory Skills

Through our senses, we gather most of our information about the world around us. The senses are a child's avenue to learning and are critical avenues for language development. The sensory skills discussed below represent the areas most important for learning. They are visual, auditory, and tactile.

Different children seem to learn better through different sensory areas. Be alert to the areas that seem to be most important for your child. Perhaps your child finds it necessary to smell and/or taste objects before he feels comfortable with them. If so, use these senses as activity springboards.

VISUAL

The visual sensory areas will be divided into four groups: color, shape, size, and distance. The suggestions for natural and structured activities in these four areas will be separated into three categories: same and different, sorting and grouping, and sequencing and recall.

It would be desirable in each of the following areas if you were to collect a number of objects and pictures that are the same and different. These can be used in the structured areas. When you begin stressing the concept of same and different, the objects or pictures should be identical (round balls of the same size and texture) except for one aspect — different colors. When the concept of isolating one descriptive aspect of objects or pictures for comparison is further developed, it will be possible to compare objects based on one aspect, even though the objects are not identical.

Color — Discriminating Same or Different

Natural

a. Folding the family laundry frequently provides an opportunity for color discrimination. Have your child help you by asking him to tell you whether two socks (washcloths,

[25]

towels, etc.) that you are sorting are the same or different. "Are the socks alike or not alike? Are they the same color? Are they both red?" etc. When he can do this, ask him whether a washcloth and a sock are the same color, or if the colors are different, etc.

b. Grocery shopping can also provide opportunities for comparison of oranges, apples, bananas, etc. Begin with red and green apples and ripe and green bananas. "Are these two apples the same or different? Are they the same color or different colors? Are they both red? I will put the two that are alike in our basket." After this seems established, use two apples and one banana. "Find the two that are alike, the same color, and we will put them in our grocery cart."

c. If you sew, many activities can be developed using spools of thread, buttons, or even material samples or squares. Again, start with all thread (or all buttons) for comparison. Then use thread, buttons, and material together, but compare them on the basis of only one aspect — for example, color.

Structured

a. Match things that are alike except for color; then match things that are not necessarily alike but are the same color. Or start simply with a game using children's blocks. You may feel as if you are a four- or five-year-old yourself, but this is all the more fun and interesting for your child. For example, you can say "A block man wanted to know which color blocks to build his house out of, so he decided to build his house out of the blocks that were the same color that he was. He asked the blocks to come one at a time so he could decide if they matched him or not."

b. Paint chips from the local hardware store or a commercial "Lotto" game with color emphasis are also easy sources of same and different objects. Try to find different ways to approach the game that will stimulate your child's imagination (as well as yours). Call it a different kind of "Concentration" if you want.

Color — Sorting and Grouping

Natural

Your child will still be doing the same task of discriminating, but it will be a bit more complicated because he will be dealing with more objects. The task is to put the objects into some sort of order. Dealing with the same three areas discussed previously (laundry, grocery shopping, and sewing), modify them as follows:

a. When sorting laundry, ask your child to put into one pile all washcloths that are the same color, all the socks that are the same color, etc. Then ask him to put all the clothes – socks, washcloths, towels, etc. – that are the same color into a pile or into the washing machine.

b. Using the situation of grocery shopping, ask your child to help sort the apples, oranges, canned goods, etc., that are the same and put them into a pile or onto a shelf. He's the "grocery store clerk."

c. Have your child place spools of thread that are the same color into a sewing box. Children seem to be particularly "taken" with buttons, especially if they can be sorted into small containers that he can see through, hold up, and shake.

Structured

a. Present your child with a pile of blocks, paint chips, or toy animals, etc., that are the same color. "All the blocks (or animals, etc.) got together for a party and they decided to play a game in groups. They all started to shout that they wanted to be in a certain group. To make it easier, they decided to group together by color. All those blocks that are the same color, that are alike, got together in one group. You put them that way." What if your child doesn't want to sort them or put them in a box, but wants to throw them? Fine, let him throw all the blocks that are the same color into one corner, and all that are another color into another corner.

b. If he seems to have difficulty getting the idea of grouping all the things that are the same color into one pile, use a sheet of construction paper to designate the area for the objects of that same color. It also might add a little extra interest. "These pieces of paper are trucks that need to be loaded with animals (or blocks) that are the same color as the truck and as each other. See if you can load the trucks with the animals that are the same color."

Color – Sequencing and Recall

The task is made more complicated at this point because your child needs to remember the order in which colors occur. It is particularly important during these activities to remember to place the objects or pictures in front of the child moving from *his* left to right. It is good in the beginning to develop a pattern of setting out the objects and to review them several times. "First, I will put out the blue ball; second, I will put out the red ball; and third, I will put out the green ball. The blue ball is here, the red ball is next, and the green ball is last; blue, red, green." (Touch or point to each ball as you name and review it.) "Now I am going to mix them up. Can we put them back the way they were? First was the . . ." It might help to let him handle the objects before they are scrambled and let him put them in order as you help and name them. As he becomes more skilled, you can ask him to close his eyes while you scramble the objects. (If three objects are too difficult, begin with two.)

Natural

a. This is an easy and fun game to play while doing house cleaning. Place pillows on the sofa in a particular order (children have a knack for constantly rearranging pillows anyway), books on a bookshelf (better work with only a few at a time initially), objects on a shelf, flowers on a windowsill, spices in a spice rack, toothbrushes in a rack, etc. Mix the objects up and let your child put them back in the original order. You can make it the "train game" if you wish. "The first red pillow is the engine, the next car (pillow) is blue, and the caboose or the last car is white." (Or you can use those same laundry socks placed in a particular order in a drawer.)

Structured

a. If you can draw and cut out a train engine, one car, and a caboose or find them in a coloring book, it can add to the interest of these games. A toy train, of course, would work ideally. Remember, the train will always be headed in a way to keep the objects presented to your child in the proper order – from left to right.

b. Play "Thief and Detective." Have a variety of different colored objects on a table or in the train. "Look at all the things on the table (begin with only three); I'll close my eyes, and you take one thing and hide it in your lap. I'm the detective, and I'll guess which one you took. Was I right? Now it is your turn to be the detective, and I will be the thief."

Shape – Discriminating Same or Different

The order of the activities for this section is the same as for color, except that emphasis is shifted to the shape of the objects or pictures. Many of the previous activities can be adapted to fit here. Your child may need some help in making the transition from color to shape. Give him additional clues, make your finger go around the object, etc.

Natural

a. Have your child help set the table and decide if the dishes are the same shape (plate and cup or plate and saucer, for example).

b. Having your child help Dad in his tool–and–work area by telling the difference between nails, screws, bolts, etc., brings Dad into one–to–one contact with the child in developing this skill area. "I need two nails to fix this board. Are these two the same shape?" Let your child hold them. Help him trace his finger around the outline initially to aid him in making the discrimination.

c. Outdoor activities can include same and different containers filled with wet sand or snow and turned upside down to form various shapes. This also gives your child the opportunity to make the shape that matches the one already there or to make a different one.

Structured

a. Using construction paper, cut various shapes (squares, circles, triangles, etc.) for use in matching activities. Begin by using two squares of the same color and one circle also of the same color, and have your child decide if the two kinds of shapes are the same or different. If your child has difficulty with this, it may be necessary to give him additional clues by making the circle a different color. Once the concept of shape is established, you can proceed as above. You can also Scotch-tape shapes to the floor and ask him to step on two that are alike, the same shape, or different.

b. Use any of a variety of household objects — boxes, cans, pencils, balls, etc. — in as many same and different activities as possible. Be sure to ask your child if he has an idea for a game or let him pick one of his favorite games that you have played before. Use any of the above objects to introduce the game of "Twins." "Twins are two people or things that look exactly alike — the same — they match. Find the twin for this shaped block." Or try "This is the Ball family. They all look alike. They went to the store, and the one Ball got lost with other shaped families. Can you help this Ball find his mother? Find the Ball that looks like him, that is the same. Yes, that's his mother; they look alike, they are both round."

c. Puzzles are a form of shape–matching. Commercial puzzles with simple shapes or objects that fit into one opening of the same shape are a good beginning.

Shape – Sorting and Grouping

Natural

a. Ask your child to participate in setting the table or putting dishes away. Putting silverware into appropriate bins is a form of sorting. Young children seem a little more eager to do this than older ones. "This is the house where the silver-ware people live. There is a place for everyone, but they have to go to their rooms. Everyone in that room is alike. Put all of the fork people into this room, knives here, and spoons here. You do it and see if they all fit into their rooms."

b. Frequently, a very helpful task in the tool or work areas of the house is to sort out a mixed–up box or bin of nails, bolts, screws, etc. A divided tool caddy or small boxes, cans, or jars make good containers for sorting. "This carpenter is in trouble. He needs to do some repairs but can't find the right parts he needs. Be his helper and sort the things that are the same shape, alike, in the boxes so he can get the job done."

Structured

a. There are some commercially made toys to help in this skill area. A mailbox with various-shaped openings and like-shaped blocks provides a sorting and grouping activity with blocks. "I want to mail my letter in the mailbox, but it doesn't seem to fit. I think it needs to go in a special place that is the same shape as my letter. Be a mailman and see how many letters you can mail. The letter must go into the hole that is the same shape that it is, that looks like it does."

b. The construction paper shapes used earlier in the discrimination and matching area can be used here in much the same manner as before. Cut holes in a shoe box or cardboard box of the same shapes as the construction paper shapes. "All of the circles (or squares, etc.) want to go home because they are tired, but they can only go in the door that is the same shape as they are. All of the round circles must go through the door that is round; the squares can only go through the square door that looks like they do. See if you can help everyone go home."

Shape — Sequencing and Recall

Natural

a. When you are cooking, line up two or three ingredients contained in the recipe you are preparing, such as in a cake — the mix box, eggs, measuring cup with water. "My recipe says first I put in the mix, second the eggs, and third the water. Here is the mix, next the eggs, and last the water — mix, eggs, water. I am going to mix them up. You be the cook and put them back in order."

b. To develop skill in this area and speed up the morning dressing time, lay out your child's clothes in the order in which he will put them on. "First you will need your socks, second your sweater, and last your pants — socks, sweater, pants. See if I can fool you and mix them up. You put them back in order."

Structured

a. "Hide and Seek" is the name of this game. Line up three objects in front of the child (left to right). "First is the box, second comes the can, third is the pencil. Here is the box, next the can, and last the pencil — box, can, pencil." Put a piece of cardboard in front of the objects (or ask him to close his eyes) and remove one of the objects. "Now help the can (or whatever) find its place with the others. Put it in order. First was the . . ." In the beginning choose the item in the center, letting the space serve as an additional clue for the child. As he becomes more adept at this skill, remove an object, but be sure that the remaining objects are together (with no space as a clue). Scramble the objects up before his eyes or behind the cardboard, and ask him to put all of them back in order. Finally, add more objects to the task until it gets too difficult for him.

b. If planting or gardening is a family interest, have him help. Children seem to love this, especially if they have a small garden of their own (fondly called a "Vegetable Soup" garden, since nothing ever seems to end up in rows). Line up the items you will need for planting: shovel for digging the hole, sprinkling can for water, and plant or bulb. Remember the review procedure: shovel, water, plant. Mix them up and ask him to put them in order. You can talk to yourself here or ask him questions, depending upon his language abilities. "Why is the shovel first? What will happen if I just set the plant on top of the ground? Does the plant need water to grow?" Answer the questions yourself if necessary.

c. Storytelling can be adapted to developing sequencing and recall skills. Choose three objects of different shapes and make up a simple story about them. "Suzie had a little black *dog.* One day she put the dog into a *box* to visit her grandmother. Her grandmother gave her a *cookie* to eat. It was good." As you read the story, place the italic objects in front of your child (left to right). Review them for him. Give him the objects and have him set them out at the proper place in the story and in the right order. You are giving him other clues and building memory skills in addition to shape sequencing. Have him put the objects in order without the story. Then let him eat the cookie, and you have a winner for a repeat activity.

Size – Discriminating Same and Different

The procedures are the same again, and emphasis is shifted to size. Be sure to give your child opportunities to hold and handle objects, especially early in the activities to provide many clues before you ask him to consider size only.

Natural

a. Cleaning up closets or dressing areas is ideally suited to discriminating and matching items on the basis of their size. Boots, coats, mittens, shoes, etc., can be matched and placed in order. Try to keep the items in order from small to large or large to small to help build the concept of sequencing for later skills. Talking to yourself is particularly appropriate here. "Daddy's boots are big. Try them on. See how big they are? Help me put Daddy's big boots here. They are the same size. Next are Mommy's boots. They are big, too, but not as big as Daddy's boots. Mommy's boots are smaller than Daddy's so they will go next, etc." Continue on through the family members.

b. The ever–continuing laundry activities also can provide opportunities for comparison by size, especially with washcloths and towels.

c. Snack time is a good comparison opportunity. Children seem to learn quickly which cookies or pieces of candy are the same or not the same. "One cookie is different, not the same size – larger than the other two. Point to it. Which cookie do you want to eat? You want the largest cookie — the cookie that is not the same as the other two."

Structured

a. Straws cut into different sizes can be used in a variety of play situations. For example, play "Ice Cream Man." "A family comes into the ice cream store, and Daddy wants a soda. We need two straws that are the same size — that match — and that are long enough for Daddy's soda. Mother wants a coke. Now we need two straws that are the same size and the right size for Mother's coke. The boy in the family wants a small orange drink. We need two straws that are the same size and small enough to fit the orange drink." It would be helpful to have containers of various sizes to be more realistic. Now ask for comparisons: "Will these two straws fit? Why not? Are they the same size? Do these two look alike?"

b. Using construction paper or newspaper (two pieces the same size), and a pair of scissors, you can work with this activity to develop size comparisons. Do a take–off on Sesame Street's "Cookie Monster." "I am a paper monster. I have two sheets of paper that are the same size; they are alike, but I like to cut up paper. That's what paper monsters do. So I will cut one sheet in two (as *exactly in two* as possible — sometimes it helps to draw the cutting lines ahead of time as guidelines). Now the two sheets are not the same size, they are not alike; but these two new ones are — they are the same size — they are alike," etc. After the pieces of paper become rather small after many cuttings, begin comparison among the different sizes.

Size — Sorting and Grouping

Natural

a. Clean and sort the magazine rack. "Put all the magazines that are the same size into a pile." Or, "Make a path using all the magazines. Then walk the path, stepping on each magazine that is the same size, but different from the other magazines. All these magazines are not the same size; this path is made from magazines that are a different size."

b. Help return dishes to the proper place in the cabinet. "The plates that are the same size stack on top of one another. These plates are a different size; they are not the same. They must have a pile of their own."

Structured

a. Using toy cars of different and the same size, and a pan of water, say "The carwash person thinks it is easier to wash all of the cars that are the same size at one time. The cars need to line up for their turn. Put all the cars that are the same size — alike — in one line and in another line put the cars that are a different size. Now wash the cars, and put all those cars that are alike in the same place to dry. These two people are coming to get their cars. Are their cars the same size or different?" The activity can be used with plastic animals, dolls, doll clothes, blocks, etc.

b. If you can find three or four golf balls and three or four tennis balls, you can set up a fun game by cutting holes in the bottom of a large box — small ones for the golf balls and larger ones for the tennis balls. Turn the box over so the holes are up and see if your child can drop the balls into the proper hole — a variation of the old "clothespins in the bottle" game.

Size — Sequencing and Recall

Natural

a. Many items in the kitchen and cooking areas lend themselves to this task, such as graduated sizes of pans, mixing bowls, measuring cups, measuring spoons, etc. Give your child an opportunity to handle and play with these items while you are at work in the kitchen. Try to get into the habit of presenting them to him in the same way. In other words, instead of simply handing them all to him out of order, show him the smallest, next, and so on to the largest, or show him how the largest one can be the holder for them all.

b. When cleaning or picking up your child's room, ask him to help and place his stuffed animals, dolls, cars, etc., on the bed, a shelf, or the floor, according to size.

Structured

a. There are many commercial nesting toys available. Show your child how they fit together, set them out in a row, stack them on top of one another from largest to smallest, etc. "The man in the circus wants to see how many people he can hold. He is very strong, and many people will get up on his shoulders; first, a large person, then a person who is a little smaller, etc."

b. It is also possible to line up members of your family according to size. Have your child close his eyes while the order is changed, and have him put the family back in order. This can be done with a doll house family also.

c. The traditional story of "Goldilocks and The Three Bears" emphasizes differences in size of bears, bowls, chairs, and beds. Reading this story and using catalog pictures as the objects in the story is motivating for some children. "Here are the three bears' beds. Which one is Papa Bear's bed? Which one is the biggest or largest of the beds? Which one is next? Which one is Mother Bear's bed?" and so on.

Distance — Discriminating Same and Different

Natural

a. Start this activity while looking out the window. This gives your child a tangible barrier as a frame of reference. Stand conveniently located and an equal distance from two windows. "The windows seem the same distance from us. Let's see how many steps it takes us to get to the windows. It is the same number of steps. The windows are a matching distance away from us. Everything we see outside, though, is a different distance from us. Everything outside is not the same distance from us as the windows. Everything outside is farther away from us than the distance to the windows. Everything we see inside, between us and the windows (remember, you must remain facing the windows as other objects in your house may indeed be farther away from you), is still another distance from us. Those things are not the same distance from us as the windows. They are closer to us than the windows."

b. The next time you are in a parking lot with lines painted on the lot pavement, you and your child might pace off the distance between lines to determine how well the workmen did at getting the lines equal distances apart. You can also talk about the distance relationship between cars, cars and signs, the ticket booth, buildings in the area, streets, etc.

Structured

a. Distance is sometimes a difficult concept for a child, so any motivators and objects with interest value should be used. Using a puppet (easily made from a paper bag) and your child's more likeable toys, structure a game for him. You and the puppet have a chair as a starting point. "Our puppet (give it a name) wants to tell everyone where to sit today. He wants Teddy to sit here (a convenient distance away), and Koala Bear to sit next to him. They are the same distance from us. Let's go back to where we started and sit on the puppet's chair and have a look at them. Now puppet thinks dolly should sit way over there (a farther distance than the bears). She is not the same distance from us as Teddy and Koala; she is farther away from us." Continue the activity with more objects if your child seems to be able to handle more. Use a wagon or car to have the animals and dolls go visiting and talk about their distance from the starting point (the puppet's chair).

Distance – Grouping and Sorting

Natural

a. When asking your child to pick up his toys, use two boxes, one close and one farther away. Play "Captain, May I" with him. "Captain says you may put Raggedy Ann in the box that is close to us, the one that is the shortest distance from us. Captain says you may put Raggedy Andy in the box that is the same distance from us as Raggedy Ann. Captain says you may put the truck in the box that is far away from us – the box that is not the same distance – the box farther away from Raggedy Ann and Andy," etc.

Structured

a. Use the puppet much the same as it was used for distance discrimination, only now ask your child to place the animals or dolls in a certain way, farther or closer to you. "This time we are at puppet's house. Let's sit down here; this is his house. Over there is another house (mark the floor with tape or use colored paper or newspaper as another house). It belongs to bear. Bear's house is very close to puppet's house. They visit together often. Way over there is another house (mark it also). It belongs to cat. Cat's house is farther away. Puppet does not visit cat's house very much because it is a long way from his house. All of the animals that come to puppet's house want to go the same distance, and they do not want to go very far. The animals want to visit someone close. Whose house do you think they will visit? The dolls want to visit someone far away. They all want to go the same distance, too, but they want it to be a long trip. Whose house do you think they will visit? You help the animals visit the 'close house' and the dolls visit the 'far house.'

Put them where you think they belong. You can talk aloud to yourself as the play develops and increase the number of houses if the task is an easy one for your child.

Distance — Sequencing and Recall

Natural

a. When taking a walk with your child, stop for a moment and ask him to name or point to a thing that is close to you; name one that is a little farther away, and so on.

Structured

a. "Statue" is a game where one child spins another. The spun child must stay where he lands, and in the same physical position. Modify "Statue" and play it with dolls or stuffed animals. "The dolls and animals want to play a game called 'Statue.' You take dolly and spin around once and let go of her. Now take Teddy and spin around twice and let go of him (your child may need help spinning); three times around for Koala. Now let's look and see where they are. Dolly is close to us, she is first; next is Teddy, and Koala is the farthest away from us. Now all of the animals come home to us. See if you can remember the order they were in. Who was the closest one to us? Dolly was first, next was . . ." Increase the number of toys until the game becomes too difficult.

b. Draw a floor diagram of your child's bedroom. Place the bed in the room for him and then have him recall the place of other objects. "What is closest to the bed? What's next?"

AUDITORY

The auditory (hearing) sensory skill is less tangible than visual; it is, however, the key to language acquisition. For a child already exhibiting some difficulty with language, auditory skills may be difficult for him to master. *If he has learned the concepts presented in the visual–skills section, such as discriminating same and different, sorting and grouping, and sequencing and recall, it can be helpful to incorporate visual activities with the auditory in the early steps.* This will help your child by giving him a tangible and familiar activity, get him "set" for the task ahead, give him additional clues for his beginning tasks, and help him realize that there is a parallel between the two areas — you are trying to help him organize sensory data in order to make it understandable and useful for him.

The procedure is from relatively simple tasks to more complex ones. It is necessary during auditory tasks to keep other noises not pertinent to the task at hand to a minimum. The auditory section will be presented as follows: (1) awareness of sound; (2) awareness of the cause–effect relationship of sound; (3) identification of sound (when a sound is present and when it is not); (4) gross sounds; (5) characteristics of sound; and (6) general introduction to the sounds of speech.

Awareness of Sound

This section is intended as a general introduction to sound – all the sounds in the child's environment. It is an ongoing skill area to be continued throughout many stages of the program.

Natural

a. "If we listen with our ears (touch your ears and your child's ears; have him touch his ears to get him cued in on the task), we hear many, many noises. We are going to be 'noise collectors' and see how many noises we can find. We are going to start right here in our house. Mom will keep a little book of all the noises we hear. I will write them down and draw a little picture of them (or cut out a picture from a magazine or catalog to paste by the noise). Then we will know how many sounds we have found. Let's start in the kitchen because there are always lots of noises there." While "collecting" sounds about the house, try to imitate them and describe them. "Swish, swish is the sound the washing machine makes. It is a slushy sound." All noises outside and on visits are sounds worth noting and talking about. "Rrum, rrum, our car makes low, loud sounds. Clank, clank is the sound the garbage people make. They are collecting garbage, and we are collecting sounds. Clank, clank is a loud sound; sometimes it hurts my ears. Tick, tick; that's our clock. It makes a sound that is quiet and soft." Invite your child to imitate the sound with you; if he will, fine. If not, let him listen to you. As you can see, this is a long–term project. Keep a notebook handy around the house and in your purse for shopping trips or visits. Make it a part of each day or several activities during the day. You will become aware of many unnoticed sounds that occur daily around your house.

b. Invite your child to a room in your house where you are working and where many sounds occur that you have collected in your book. Play "What am I?" You should make the sounds that you used to imitate the noise and describe it, too, if you wish. See if your child can find the thing in the room that you are trying to imitate. "Ring, ring is the sound I make. I am a high sound. What am I? That's right; I'm a telephone and I go ring, ring. Ruff, ruff is the sound I make. It is a (high or low) sound, and it is loud. What am I? Right, I'm Puffy the dog, and I say ruff, ruff." You can easily play this game while walking, bus riding, etc., by using outside, environmental noises.

Structured

a. Sit down with your child and one of the "collecting" notebooks with pictures. Play the "What am I?" game as above and have your child point to what he thinks you are. (If your child always guesses wrong, and ruff, ruff is the clock, and tick, tick is the toilet flushing, don't give up the collecting business; remember, you are in the business together.) If he seems to be having a great deal of difficulty, limit your questions to two or three very familiar sounds and objects; make the sound, and ask the question, "What am I?" Take him by the hand and say "I will show you who I am." Have him touch the object and make the sound; you make the imitated sound, and use it in a sentence with the sound. "Blub, blub is the sound I make. I am a low, quiet sound. What am I? I'll show you what I am (take him to the object). I am the water in the bathtub as it goes down. Blub, blub; hear the sound I make. Let's listen together to the real sound (put water in the tub). Hear the blub, blub as the water goes down. Blub, blub is the sound I make when I am water going down the drain. Blub, blub. What am I? Let's make the blub, blub sound together. Now we are both water in the bathtub."

b. If you have a tape recorder, use it in very much the same way.

c. List all the sounds you hear people making: talking, singing, whispering, laughing, coughing, sneezing, sighing, snoring, clapping hands, stomping feet, etc. You can come up with quite a long list in a very short time.

Awareness of the Cause–Effect Relationship of Sound

This relationship exists in several ways: (1) action followed by sound (push the doorbell, and ding, dong occurs); (2) action and sound occurring at the same time (stamp your feet going up the stairs, and clump, clump occurs at the same time); (3) sound followed by action ("I want a cookie," usually results in a cookie in the hand and subsequently in the mouth). Although it is easier to find examples of the first two relationships, it is the third one, sound that brings about a result, that is basic to language.

Natural

a. Overdramatize cause–and–effect sounds about the house. Every time you come in the door, make an exaggerated motion of ringing the doorbell, cup your hand to your ear and listen. "I hear ding, dong after I push the doorbell. I push the bell (push it again), then I hear the sound. You do it now. Push the bell. Listen. Do you hear the sound?" Do this with many objects throughout the house, such as electric mixers, hair dryers, vacuum cleaners, child's talking dolls or animals, etc.

b. Using a toy drum or box and a wooden spoon, beat on the drum and say "Hear the boom, boom sound the drum makes when I hit it: boom, boom. You make the drum go boom, boom. Listen to the sound it makes." Now take the spoon or drumstick and beat on a pillow. "The pillow doesn't go boom, boom. No boom. You hit the pillow. No boom. Now hit the drum. Yes, that's the boom, boom. Only the drum will go boom, boom. You are a fine drummer."

c. Expecting your child to use the language he has – to get what he wants – is one of the best ways to make him aware that sounds will bring results. Some verbalization within his ability level should be encouraged before granting wishes. More is said about this in a later section on language.

Structured

a. If you can find a small bell and a clicker, you can play a game in which the players raise their hands each time the bell is rung and put their hands down each time the clicker clicks. It becomes kind of a "Simon Says" to sounds.

b. Several games could be set up so that the response depends upon some sound being present. Place a few blocks between you and your child and then set an egg timer to one minute or less. When the timer goes off, the person to pick up the most blocks wins.

Identification of Sound — Awareness of When
a Sound Is Present and When It Is Not Present

This is a good time to begin introducing the gross sounds to be used later for discrimination. Begin collecting small noisemakers with a variety of characteristics: high–low, loud–soft, pleasant–unpleasant, etc. You can find many of these things about the house, and most children find great delight in making their own noisemakers. Some toys you might collect include: drum, talking dolls or animals, bell, whistle, Halloween noisemakers, lids from two pans, baby rattles, etc. Try to collect two or more of each object for use in later activities. In order to get two objects with the same sound, it is sometimes easier to make noisemakers using boxes, jars, cans, plastic containers, etc., with various numbers of different objects in them. Placing objects such as marbles, rocks, cotton, pieces of paper, macaroni, rice, sugar, pins, buttons, crayons, dry cereals, bells, small toys, etc., inside will increase your child's interest in the activity. The task here is to use any of the noisemakers and ask your child to raise his hand (or march, wiggle, color a picture, hold up a picture or object) or otherwise respond physically when he hears a particular sound and to keep doing that activity as long as he hears the sound. He should stop the activity when the sound stops.

Natural

a. Let your child use a toy vacuum and "help" you do the cleaning. "Come help Mom clean up the house. We are going to vacuum. My vacuum makes the vvrum sound. Hear it? (Momentarily start the vacuum.) This can be your vacuum (toy or pretend). You make it go when you hear the vacuum noise. Let's practice it first. I'll make the noise and you vacuum. That's right, and when I stop the noise, you stop vacuuming. You are a dandy helper."

b. Use noise–producing objects or appliances in the house in much the same manner. An electric mixer, for instance, can be used in this way: "Help me make a cake. You mix with your spoon and bowl when I make the mixer sound. When the mixer sound stops, you stop mixing." Use an electric razor or a hair dryer, or simply make a noise with one of the noisemakers mentioned earlier and ask him to help you pretend something.

Structured

a. "Musical Chairs" comes to mind as a game that teaches awareness to the presence or absence of sound. It was used earlier in a similar activity. Play it first alone with your child and then enlist the help of other family members or friends. "We are going to play 'Musical Chairs.' I will set some chairs in a circle. When you hear a sound (a noisemaker, the radio, television, or record player), you walk around the chairs. As soon as the sound stops, you quietly find a chair and sit down in it. I'll practice it with you, and then you do it alone."

b. A type of "Blind Man's Bluff" can provide another opportunity for identification of sound. Play the game first without a blindfold until the child seems to have the idea and is able to respond most of the time. "We are going to play 'Blind Man's Bluff.' If you were blind and you could not see, you would have to be a good listener to help you walk around and find things. If I take this bell to the corner of the room and ring it, you can hear the ringing sound. Listen. Do you hear it? (Make the sound.) See if you can point to where you hear the sound. That's right. Now close your eyes, and I am going to move to another place in the room. Keep your eyes closed (or blindfolded); listen, now point to where you hear the sound." This activity not only teaches awareness to the presence or absence of sound, but it also develops another listening ability, that of localizing sound or picking out the direction from which a sound is coming.

Gross Sounds – Discrimination

It is hoped that the concept of same and different has been learned by your child to the degree that he is able to indicate to you by verbalizing such terms as same or different, yes or no, alike or not alike, in order to indicate his judgment of two things. In its pure form, gross sound discrimination should be a listening task only. However, at this point it may be necessary to give your child some visual clues to begin his listening task. The procedure for discriminating sound is the same as with visual objects. Collect two or three of each type of sound–making object.

Natural

a. Initially, choose your sounds carefully so that the two alike sounds that you will present will also be alike visually, and the one that sounds different also looks different. Once your child has mastered this task, then you can begin to remove some of the visual clues and make it purely an auditory or listening task. When you are involved in an activity using dishes or mixing bowls or pans, the opportunity is there for developing this listening task. "You are becoming such a good listener! You are keeping me busy finding lots of sounds for us to listen to. Let's see, if we use some of the dishes we have out here, I bet that we can be a band. The band leader needs a stick to help the band. We will let this spoon be the band leader's stick. If I tap this glass gently, it makes a sound. Listen. Hear the sound the glass makes? Now I will tap this other glass gently (same size, shape, color); it makes the same sound. Listen to the two sounds together. They sound the same. These two glasses can play together in the band. They sound just alike. You tap these two glasses gently and listen to them make the same sound. Hear it? They sound the same. Now let's tap the plate. Listen to the sound it makes. It's a different sound than the one the glasses make. Let's listen to them both (tap glasses, then plate). They do not sound alike; they sound different. I guess we will let the plate play in the band, but he had better play away from the two glasses. The two glasses sound the same (tap each), but a glass and a plate sound differently (tap each)." If your child can tell the difference with ease, try having him close his eyes and have him tell you which two you tapped, and if they sounded the same or different.

b. Once your child does not need visual clues to help him in his listening task, many opportunities arise for discriminating sounds. You can begin to make the sounds even more alike. Admittedly, many of the sounds you find may sound differently. Finding the ones that are the same may be the fun of it. Many birds repeat the same tune over and over; compare that tune to a dog's bark, or – if your child seems to be doing an especially good job of discriminating – compare the tunes of two birds (a more difficult task). A stick, striking two fence posts, may sound the same, but a fence post and the gate may sound differently. If you gently tap two large windows, they may sound alike, but a large window and a small one will sound differently. Two large rocks dropped in the water may sound alike, but a large rock and a stick will be different.

Structured

a. Now is the time to get out all those noisemakers to play "Sound Password." The noisemakers come to the door two by two to see if they can enter the secret hiding place of the Grand Noisemaker of them all. Give it all you've got and try to add a little secretiveness to the situation. Turn down the

the lights if you wish; have your child (the Grand Noisemaker of them all) sit inside a large cardboard box or under a table. "Both of the noisemakers must make the same sound for the password, or they will not be allowed to enter. Here are the first two. Listen to the sounds they make. Do you hear the same sound or different sounds? Listen again. Do these two fellows sound alike or different? Yes, they are alike. They sound the same. They can both come in. Two more are coming. Listen! Do they both have the same password? Listen one more time. No, they do not sound the same. They have different passwords."

b. Play "Sesame Street" with your child. Many children are at least familiar with the format and some of the songs from "Sesame Street." You may even have some of the characters from the show in toy form to help along with the game. "We can make one of the Sesame Street songs to be a sound song. (Place three noisemakers on the table or floor — two alike, one different.) Remember the song they sing about the pictures? We can sing it about sounds. One of these sounds is not like the others, one of these sounds just doesn't belong. . . . Listen to each one. Which one is different? Which ones are the same?" Use different noisemakers for the next turn, and as your child develops the skill, use more than three at a time.

Gross Sounds — Sequencing and Recall

For gross sounds, we have omitted the step of sorting and grouping as used in visual discrimination because the two senses are not parallel. The duration of the sensory stimulation is different. In other words, a red block sitting on a table is red all the time and can be picked up and moved while it is still being red. If you ring a bell, however, the bell is still there, but the sound of the ringing bell only lasts a short time, and then it is gone. In order to compare the sound of the bell with another sound, one stops before the other begins. You could continue ringing the bell while making another sound at the same time, but this makes the task a much more difficult one. It becomes a task akin to picking out the sound of a musical instrument in a band or orchestra.

Natural

a. Most household objects will make varying sounds when tapped, knocked or banged. When cleaning or even when sitting where furniture or objects are nearby, use this opportunity to build the skill of sequencing and recalling sounds. Your child must have the opportunity to hear and identify the sounds you are going to use first before he can be expected to sequence them, so review them often for him. "Let's play a guessing game with sounds. We'll call it our 'Choo–Choo Train of Sound.' I am going to let this table be first this time. It can be the engine of our train. Let's listen to the engine (knock on the table). Hear the sound it makes? That's the first sound (make it again). You make the engine make its sound. You knock on the table and make the first sound. I hear it. I know what it sounds like. Let's make the chair be next. Let's listen to it (knock on upholstered chair). It makes a different, quiet sound. It sounds different than the table. Let's listen to them again. The table sound is first; the chair sound is next. You make them and listen. First the table; next the chair. Now close your eyes while I make them and just listen. Point to the first sound I make; now point to what was next. Now I am going to mix them up." You might let him keep his eyes open at first until he is responding well, then have him close his eyes. "Now we are going to add on to the train. We need another sound. You pick one. The window makes a good sound when we knock on it. Let's listen to the sounds we have again: the table, the chair, and the window." (Make the sounds as you name each one.) If your child has difficulty sequencing the sounds with his eyes closed, tell him how you have changed them and let him listen again. When he does get them right, let him know it, and review them for him. "Yes, that's right; the table, the chair, and the window." Add on as many sounds as he seems able to handle.

b. Nearly every household task involves a sequence of sounds. What sounds are involved in getting a glass of milk? First, the refrigerator door is opened, then the milk carton is removed, the door closed, a glass is taken from the cupboard, the milk is poured, etc. Point out how the sounds tell a story. Talk through the sequence with your child.

Structured

a. Use noisemakers to make a storm. "We are going to sound out a storm. First, it is quiet right before the storm. The first sound is a quiet one. Listen to it (any quiet sound — cotton in a plastic container, for example). That is the sound before the storm. Next comes the wind, soft at first, and then louder. This is the sound the wind makes. (Noisemaker for the wind can be a whistle or plastic lid with a few holes punched in it and rapidly waved in the air.) First, the quiet before the storm (make the sound), next the wind (make the sound), now the thunder and lightning (two metal lids, drum, rocks in a can, etc.) Listen to the sound of the thunder! First, the quiet before the storm, next the wind, then the thunder and lightning (make each sound), and last the rain (rice, beans, sugar, etc., in a can or plastic container). Listen to the rain; the storm is here. Let's listen to them all again (review). Now I am going to leave one out. You guess which one is not there." Make them while he is watching and leave out thunder and lightning. "Which sound of the storm did I forget?" Continue the game, and have him close his eyes and listen only. Leave out a different sound each time. Remember, he might like a chance to be the storm and you listen. As he becomes more skilled at this, you can omit more than one sound, have him put them all in order, or play "mixed–up" storm (it rains first, then thunder and lightning, etc.).

b. Use the more musical noisemakers for this activity, which we call "Here Comes the Band." A little marching and fanfare helps. The procedure is the same as above: "We are playing 'Here Comes the Band' today. The first instrument in the band is the horn (whistle, tambourine, etc.). Listen to it. You make the sound. Next comes the drum," and so on, reviewing them all as you add on, as above. See if your child can guess which sound is missing. Have him put them in order using two or more instruments, or let him guess the mixed–up order of three or four instruments.

Characteristics of Sounds

This area is intended to develop awareness, identification, and discrimination of the descriptive qualities of sound, such as (1) loud–soft, high–low, long–short, and identification of voices. During the course of this section, try to put a great deal of vocal variety into your own voice, not just while you are thinking of language work, but at all times. Use the whole gamut of your voice in terms of loud and soft, high and low, slow speech, and rapid speech.

Awareness of Loud and Soft Sounds

Natural

a. Begin a systematic attempt to call your child's attention to loud and soft sounds. Begin with only loud sounds and refer to all others as being not loud. "The siren is loud. It is so loud it hurts my ears. It is a high, loud sound. The thunder is loud. A storm is coming. The thunder is low and loud. This house is noisy. My ears tell me the noise in this house is loud." Try to describe the sound in addition to identifying what is making the sound and saying that it is loud.

b. Introduce soft, quiet sounds: "The kitten makes a soft, quiet, purring sound. It is a low, gentle sound. Take a deep breath. Breathing in and out makes a quiet sound. Your breath sounds like soft wind blowing. The refrigerator makes a quiet, low sound. Listen to its soft sound."

c. Now begin identifying sounds as either loud or soft as they occur. Make comparisons of sounds, but remember, not all sounds are loud or soft; some are in between and are neither loud nor soft. If he begins identifying sounds as loud or soft to you, great! Let him tell you, but this is primarily a task for you. Use noises you are able to manipulate here, such as the radio, television, record player, tape recorder, etc.

Structured

a. Choose the noisemakers that you have used previously and/ or that your child has particularly enjoyed and that can be easily varied in loudness for a game of "Lion and Kitten." It might be helpful or more fun for your child if you also happened to have a stuffed or plastic lion, or kitten, or a picture of each, to help him identify loud sounds with the lion and soft ones with the kitten. "Here is our lion. He makes loud, big sounds when he roars and walks (demonstrate the lion's roar and clump–clump walk and make your voice loud as you talk about the lion); and here is our kitten. The kitten is soft, and he makes soft, little, quiet sounds when he purrs and mews and walks (demonstrate a quiet kitten; use a quiet voice when talking about the kitten). We are going to listen and pretend we are walking down a path in the forest. We hear a sound, and we need to decide if it is a lion – loud and big – or if it is a kitten – soft, little, and quiet. Let's practice being the loud lion first (demonstrate: let him make any loud noise, roar, jump, walk heavily, etc.). Now let's practice the kitten (demonstrate kitten)." Let him watch you at first while you make a noise with one of the noisemakers and help him identify by pointing, demonstrating (running if it's the lion, petting if it's the kitten), or naming the animal he thinks made the sound. When this seems fairly easy, ask him to turn his back or go behind a piece of furniture to listen to the sound.

b. Let your child have an opportunity now to make loud and soft sounds. He has had much practice with the loud ones. With the soft ones, he may need a little help. Use the lion and kitten objects or pictures from the above game and a drum, pot or pan with a lid or spoon, two metal lids, or any series of musical–like instruments or noisemakers that can be varied from soft to loud. "We are in the Land of Noise. All of the things that live here make a noise of one kind or another. They like to make noise, but they have trouble sometimes deciding whether to make a loud or a soft noise. You see, Noiseland has two kings: One is a lion, and he likes loud, big noises; and one is a kitten, and he likes soft, quiet noises. This chair is the throne of the king. When the lion is sitting on the throne, the things that live here make only loud noises. When the kitten is king and sitting on the throne, the things make only soft, quiet noises. Let's try it. You may pick any of the noisemakers to please the king. What sound will it make when the lion is king? (Use a loud voice for a clue.) Now the kitten is king (change the picture or object). Make a game of it. Change them obviously at first, then have him watch for the change, or make it a quick one.

Awareness of High– and Low–Pitched Sounds

It is very helpful, while working on this skill, to have musical instruments of some sort at hand. A piano, horn, or a stringed instrument, of course, can provide a wide range of pitches, but children's musical instruments, such as play piano, xylophone, bells of different pitches, or glasses filled to different levels with water, provide enough pitch variation to make them useful in developing this area and are sufficient.

Natural

a. If you have a piano or other musical instrument (toy or real), take a few minutes to introduce awareness of high and low sounds. Begin with low sounds and refer to all other sounds as "not low" (initially), and keep the pitches far apart. "Listen to this low sound. It sounds 'way down' to me. It is a low sound. See if you can make a low sound. This sound (make a high one) is not low, but this one (make a low sound) is way down low. You can sing the low sounds, too (hum the sound)." If your child imitates the low sound with his voice, praise him, but remember this is primarily a listening task.

b. During the daily activity of clearing the dinner table of dirty dishes, fill the cleared glasses with different levels of water (if it happens to be colored water, all the better: try leftover coffee, tea, or Kool-Aid, or add food coloring). Set the glasses in order, from filled-to-the-top to no water at all. Take a spoon and tap the glasses gently while talking about high sounds. "We can make the glasses make music. If I tap them gently with the spoon (tap the empty glass), it makes a pretty sound. It is a high-up sound. You tap the glass and make the high sound. This one is not as high (tap the full glass)." You can begin to use high and low together, if he seems to grasp the concept, and make the comparison of which glass sounds high and which one sounds low. Call the low-pitched glass (full one) the "man" and the high-pitched glass (empty) the "woman" if this seems to help your child make the proper association. Of course, helping to fill and pour out the glasses is half of the fun.

Structured

a. If you do not own a musical instrument, don't run out and buy one; make one. Take a fairly wide cut of board and a bag of rubber bands. Stretch one of the rubber bands to its maximum length (without breaking it). Measure that distance and place two thumbtacks on the board that distance apart and stretch the rubber band over them. That begins the high sounds. Place two more thumbtacks next to these but slightly closer together, and so on, until you have a harp-like instrument. Proceed with an activity as described above with the piano.

b. If your child seemed to respond well to the activity of associating the lion and kitten with loud and soft sounds, use the same concept for pitch. How about an elephant for low and a mouse for high? "We are going to listen to high sounds (again vary your own voice high) and low sounds to play a game called 'Mountain and Valley.' Let's take your stuffed (or plastic) animals (or dolls, etc.), and let them play, too. We will use this upside-down box for the mountain, and the floor will be the valley. The animals live here on a ranch (a box or sack). These animals are good listeners. When they hear a high-pitched sound like this (demonstrate on instrument or with voice), they can go to the mountain to find food. When they hear a low sound (demonstrate), they can go to the valley to drink water. You pick an animal, and we will practice. Listen to the sound." Let your child see you make the sound at first and use only the high and low ends of your instrument. After he seems to be responding well, make the sounds behind a chair and have him listen only. Go through the animals in the sack one at a time and have him decide whether they go to eat or drink.

Awareness of Long and Short Sounds

Language has a rhythm to it, and the length of sounds and the length of no sounds (pauses) help contribute to that rhythm.

Natural

a. If you have a three–speed record player, use it to introduce the concept of duration of sound. Play a portion of a favorite simple child's record at normal speed. Now turn the speed to a more rapid or slower setting. Talk about the differences. It is possible to slow down a record by placing your finger gently on the rotating disc. Let your child make quick movements to the speeded–up record and slow movements to the slowed–down record. Activities such as running, moving arms, making sounds, etc., work well. In addition, he may like the idea of associating the various movements with animals, such as a slow elephant and a rapid, busy beaver.

b. Do you have a buzzing alarm clock? Let it run for extra long periods some mornings, and tell your child that some days a long sound is needed to wake you up. Set the alarm again and turn it off right away to illustrate a short sound. Point out long and short sounds with other familiar noises, such as the car horn, egg timer, etc.

Structured

a. Cut a number of pieces of paper into long and short strips. Ask your child to color them. The long strips are worms, and the short ones are bugs. "We are going to listen to long worm sounds (draw out your voice, too) and short bug sounds. The long worms live here (designate an area), and the short bugs live here under a rock. When the long worms hear a long sound, they may come out and explore. When you hear a long sound, you may help one of the worms come out. When you hear a short sound, help one of the bugs come out." Place the worms in their "home" by lining up the papers and making a long sustained sound while running your finger along each worm as he is placed "home."

Do the opposite with the bugs as they are placed under their rock. Now your child begins to listen to the long or short sounds you make with your voice, or noisemaker. He must decide whether a worm or a bug can come out to explore.

b. Use the same strips of paper from above and play "SOS Morse Code." "We are on an island and cannot get off. We hope if we use a special combination of long and short sounds called Morse Code, and write them in the sand, an airplane will come by and save us. We need to try different combinations of sounds until we get the right one. First, we'll try one long sound and two short ones. This is what they will look like in the sand. One long (run your finger over a long strip while making a long sound) and two short (tap your finger on short strips while making a short sound). Now you try it." Use other combinations of sounds, and add one or two more sounds if this seems to be a reasonable task for him.

Identification of Voices

This is usually a most enjoyable activity, since it is best carried out in a natural situation with other members of the family and/or friends.

Natural

a. Systematically point out how you can identify people by the way they sound. "That's Daddy in the kitchen; I can tell from his deep voice. I know Grandma's voice right away; it just sounds like Grandma."

b. During a family conversation, have everyone close his eyes and listen hard to each person's voice. As the conversation goes on, make a comment about each person's speaking voice. Do some comparing of voices and try to imitate them.

Structured

a. Start by having two family members stand or sit next to one another so that your child can see them. Silly sayings or parts of funny stories can be used. Ask your child to point to the person who is speaking, or name him if he wishes. Next, ask the two family members to stand in another room or hold a newspaper in front of their faces while one reads a portion of a story or says something. Then the child is asked to identify who was speaking. Add family members as the task becomes comfortable to your child.

b. The above activity can be made more difficult by blindfold-ing your child and asking him not only to identify the person who is speaking but also to point in the direction from which the person's voice is coming (in other words, localize the sound). Family members should move about the room. Re-member, your child might like an opportunity to be on the other side, so another member of the family should be blind-folded for short intervals.

Although persons' voices are somewhat altered on the tele-phone, it is a good activity to call your child on the phone (and ask other family members to do the same). See whether your child can identify who is calling. Be sure to say enough so he can determine who it is. A "hello" — and then a long pause — has often left most of us wondering which of our friends was on the other end of the line.

Introduction to Speech Sounds

The English language has thirty-eight sounds in it. Each sound is distinctly different from the other, and the ability to hear the various sounds and tell them apart is a very important skill. We do not intend to have you conduct an elaborate speech-sound-listening program, but we will provide a few introductory ideas that you can use to make your child more aware of the sounds of speech.

Isolate Speech Sounds

Isolate some speech sounds and say them by themselves (not in words) for listening purposes. Remember, we are talking about sounds and not letters.

Natural

a. Identify several household tasks with a certain sound and try to remember to make that sound each time you are doing the task. Examples would be making the /mmm/ sound as you iron, or /sh/ sound as you peel potatoes, or /p/ sound as you pop popcorn, or /r/ sound as you wash off the table-cloth. The sound doesn't have to have a natural relationship with the activity, since the goal is to get your child to hear sounds all by themselves.

b. Try to identify as many sounds of speech as you can which have meaning all by themselves and point them out. For ex-ample, oh and oo are good ones; ah after a good drink of pop; sh for quiet; mmm, that was good; and so on.

Structured

a. Find five objects or pictures which could be identified with a certain sound — /r/ for fire engine, /s/ for snake, /z/ for an electric razor (or sleeping), /f/ for an angry cat, and /t/ for a clock. Show the child the various pictures and say the accompanying sounds. After he is very familiar with each combination of picture and sound, see whether he can identify the correct picture when you make one of the sounds. Make a game, "Lost and Found," to play. Your child is the clerk at the Lost and Found office and has the picture. You have lost something and come in to make the sound. If he wants to reverse roles and make the isolated sounds — fine. Let him do it.

b. No doubt you read a good deal to your child. Next time you read a story, go through the book and find some places where isolated sounds would fit into the story. For example: in a story about trains, the /ch/ sound could be put in whenever there is a reference to the train; or, change the name of the story character to be an isolated sound and use it throughout the story. Many objects could have a certain sound assigned to them, too.

Scrapbook of Sound

The purpose of this activity is to continue awareness of speech sounds and to give your child an opportunity to hear a particular designated sound in a number of words.

Natural

a. In your day-to-day routine, you might make a mental scrapbook of sound. This can eventually lead to the development of a scrapbook that you and your child can make together. First, select a "Speech Sound of the Week." For example, /p/ would be a good sound to use. Now your task is to try to find as many items as possible around the house that start with that sound. Emphasize the sound and try for as much stimulation of the sound as you can muster. The goal is to bombard your child with the target sound, not necessarily to get him to say it. Try for sentences with extra /p/ sounds — "Please put the pan down." After a few days of trying to zero in on this one sound, it is time to move to a more structured approach.

Structured

a. First, buy an inexpensive scrapbook or make one by punching holes along the sides of construction paper. Now you are ready to begin the search for pictures of things that begin with the target sound, /p/. Old magazines or catalogs are "gold mines." Go through magazines with your child and name each of the pictures. When you find one that starts with the target sound, make a "big deal" of it. Then cut out the picture and place it on the /p/ page. Some talking to yourself will help here. "Let's see, we are looking for words that start with /p/ (not *pee*, just p); coat . . . c . . . oa . . .t; nope. Pie . . . p . . . ie; yes, I hear it . . . pie. Let's cut this one out and paste it on the /p/ page. This is a picture of a pie. The pie looks good. I think it's apple pie." Change sounds once you feel each one has been well covered. Remember, don't ask your child to say the sounds, or even to decide if the words start with the sound; you do all of the work at this time, and he will learn from you.

TACTILE

Touch and Muscle Sense

Two sensory skill areas are involved in the following activities: touch, or tactile; and muscle sense, or kinesthetic. This area is designed to heighten your child's sensitivity to sensory information received by feeling experiences. The various sensory experiences we suggest as possible areas for training include: soft–hard, smooth–rough, wet–dry, cold–hot (or maybe warm), light–heavy, and identification of shape or configuration of objects. For the purposes of the following discussion, they will be grouped, and the suggested activities can be adapted as you wish.

Natural

a. As with other areas, you begin with your environment and find as many examples of a given target area (for example, soft–hard) as possible. "Your pillow is soft. Feel the soft bed. The wall is not soft." Initially, use the terms "soft" and "not soft" before you begin to use *soft* and *hard* together.

d. During mealtime, try talking about soft foods (mashed potatoes, for instance). Have your child tell you if a food placed in his mouth while his eyes are closed is soft, or not soft, and later, soft or hard. See if he can identify by name or point to the food on his plate.

Structured

a. Introduce the idea of a "feeling bag or box" to your child. It is a bag or box of things to feel but not to see. Place five or six familiar objects in a bag and have your child reach in to touch and identify them. You may have to have duplicate objects for him to point to on the table in order for him to tell you what he is feeling since he may not have the vocabulary to name a horse or man, etc. "Reach in the bag and find something. Feel it — all around — turn it over in your hand. Do you see that thing (or a picture of the thing) on the table? Point to it (or name it)." Make it a detective or secret agent game, if that will help. He is looking for clues in the bag to solve the mystery. Sometimes turning down the lights will help focus in on the "feeling only" concept.

b. Placing objects under the blankets, or under sheets on a bed and playing "Undercover" can turn into a lively game. The idea is to focus on one of the skill areas from the previous list and have your child "find all of the undercover things that are light or heavy, etc., and identify what they are." Taking the object out from under the covers after naming it is usually a delightful experience.

PART III:

Language Development

How do children learn language? We really don't know. Conflicting theories abound, and the "experts" have very few answers. Language is decidedly man's most complex human activity. Yet most children appear to learn the system in a matter of a few years without formal instruction.

Speaking involves coordination of the musculature of the breathing mechanism, the voice–producing mechanism, and the throat and mouth. Although clear and articulate speech is a goal that all parents set for their children, there is an even more important task: learning the rules that govern our language system.

Language learning is essentially rule learning, since there are sets of rules that govern all parts of language. Strange as it may seem, parents "teach" these rules to their children even though neither parent nor child could state the rules if they had to. With that in mind, it really isn't so strange that some children have difficulty learning speech and language; rather, it appears strange that children are able to learn the system at all.

In the following section of this book we will present some suggestions for developing your child's speech and language systems. Don't worry, however, for we are not going to take you back to your high school English class and make you diagram sentences. The procedures that follow will be fun and productive.

GENERAL SUGGESTIONS

Six general suggestions will form the nucleus of your work on language development. These six points are crucial, and you should be sure that they are clearly understood since they will be incorporated into all future discussions.

Most language experts agree that these are the most important environmental ingredients in a child's language learning, and if we can point them out to you and give you concrete suggestions for applying them with your child, the chances for accelerated language development are excellent.

I: Model the Correct Language Target

It should go without saying that a child will not learn his language system if he is never exposed to it, and yet parents vary greatly in how much talking they do around their children. If your house is not a particularly verbal one and if your child is having some difficulty learning to talk, you should make a conscious effort to talk more. Although some parents find this simple request very demanding, you should take inventory now of just how much language your child is exposed to each day.

If you have a tape recorder, you could engage in an intriging experiment. Without people knowing it, record a lively family conversation. Play the tape back and listen for the number of started sentences that never reached completion, the number of sentences begun and then restated in a new way, interruptions, abbreviated statements, aside statements, and moments when more than one person is talking. *This is the language model for your child.*

You may not want to change the way in which your family communicates with one another in lively conversation, but it may be helpful to set aside some time each day when you can provide your child with some easier language models. Moments of controlled, one–to–one communication with your child may provide him with excellent models of language. Find time to do this as often as possible.

Probably the best language stimulation is the talking that goes on between parent and child where some *problem–solving* is involved. Such everyday tasks as trying to loosen a tight jar lid, finding a lost pair of scissors, deciding what to have for lunch, or determining which television show to watch include three crucial ingredients for language learning: a problem to be solved, a verbal description of the problem and options for solving the problem, and a resulting action that clearly reflects the verbal discussion. You will be surprised how many times each day you solve small problems without even discussing them. Try to get in the habit of putting your thoughts into words, since this allows your child to compare what he sees as the problem with what he hears you describe, and with what he sees you carry out as a plan of action to solve the problem.

As language develops, mutual problem–solving − with the child being encouraged to make suggestions − is a key ingredient in furthering language growth. You may find it effective to act upon many of the child's suggestions so that he can see the outcome of his ideas.

Strive for a variety of language behaviors when talking with your child. We have found that there is a tendency among parents to restrict their language samples to very simple utterances, all with a similar format. An example would be the parent who plays with her child in the following manner: "Here is a duck. Here is a pig. Here is a truck. Here is a boat." Although this may be good vocabulary building, it is not what we are after in modeling language for the child.

The general goal is to provide a wide variety of language types (sentence types) for the child to hear. (Later in our discussion we will talk about isolating language rules and we will suggest that you become rather restricted in what types of language you use; but these two suggestions are not contradictory, they are simply directed at different goals.)

A better example of that parent–child conversation would go as follows: "Here is a duck; ducks go quack, quack. The pig is big and fat. Is he pink? I think so. I saw a pig on a farm. Where is Mother Pig? There she is!" No doubt your child is already being exposed to a rich language sample, but make sure. Be a good language model.

II: Expand Your Child's Statements Into More Complex Ones

One of the most crucial things a parent can do to help a child learn language is to build his immature statements into more mature ones. This general process, called "expansion," appears to be an easy and uncomplicated process for most parents.

If your child is having some difficulty with speech and language learning, however, you might take a look at what you are doing and attempt to improve your efforts. We are convinced that expansion is most productive for language–delayed children if it is done in a certain way. When the child says "Billy up," and Mother wants him to say "Please, Mother, Billy wants to get up," she has expanded a simple request. However, she may have expanded it to such a complex statement that the ultimate goal is simply too difficult for the child to comprehend and/or incorporate. How about expanding the utterance to "Billy wants up," or "Please pick Billy up."

What we are saying is this: expand your child's statements into sentences or phrases just *slightly* more complex than his attempt. In this way you will be giving him a target that he is able to understand and imitate.

A word of caution is needed here regarding expansion. It is important that you realize that you are expanding your child's statements, not correcting him. Just give your child the opportunity to hear a more mature example of what he said. If you get into the habit of saying, "No, not more drink; say 'I want a drink!'" you are using correction rather than expansion. Similarly, you are not asking your child to say it as you did.

Don't expect him to follow your statement with the correct or expanded phrase. He will do that when his language–learning capabilities develop. Your goal is gradual progress and not immediate change. Keep this in mind, since you are a language model and not a language teacher.

Expansion is something you can do continuously throughout the day. It calls for no real effort on your part, and we think you will be surprised how naturally and easily you can do it. Some examples may help:

Child: Doggie up.
Parent: The doggie wants to get up.
Child: Daddy, bye bye.
Parent: Daddy is going bye bye.
Child: No take candy, Billy!
Parent: Don't take the candy, Billy!
Child: He a cat, too?
Parent: Is he a cat too? Yes, he is a cat.

Sometimes the most difficulty comes in self–reference statements, and there are plenty in children's speech. Although you will surely fall prey to what seems like an old joke, it is best to keep trying. Example:

Child: Me want outside!
Parent: I want to go outside.
Child: Me want outside too.

Don't give up . . .

Not all early word–like utterances by young children are really intended as a word. Baby may say "dada" as a part of sound play, not really meaning to name anyone. Sometimes parents are able to make the most of this happy accident by responding to the child as if his intentions were to talk – putting words in the child's mouth. The end result may be that the child learns to say some early words purely be accident, and some of those words may not be exactly as you might hear in adult speech. We all know of instances where children's special words (e.g., "badaw" for blanket) have become a family trade-mark. The secret these parents learned is that the exact sound accuracy is not so important as the discovery by the child that the sounds he makes have meaning.

Most of the time when children say words, they do so for a particular purpose. At this early stage, words are spoken for the following purposes:

1. to name things (e.g., either specific people, objects, or animals; or general group words)
2. to answer parental questions (e.g., "What's that? Cow.")
3. to request action (e.g., "Up!")
4. to call someone ("Mom!")
5. to echo someone else's words
6. to give a greeting ("Hi!")
7. to play with speech for one's own enjoyment

With this in mind, you may wish to listen more carefully to the words your child says to see what the whole sentence is that might be intended.

III: Keep the Thought Process Going With a Side Comment on the Child's Statement

This simple idea is a powerful one, and with a little practice, even older brothers and sisters can become master language help-ers. Build upon the statement of your child and add a little of your own thought to it. Your response to your child's state-ment should contain his original statement plus an offshoot. Here are some examples:

Child: Truck broke.
Parent: The truck is broken; it looks funny.
Child: Doggie up.
Parent: The doggie got up; Cindy is a fat dog.
Child: More soup, please?
Parent: May I have some some more soup? The soup is hot and good.

No doubt the actual language stimulation helps develop your child's language — but we have a feeling that there is an even more important factor. By building on your child's statement, you are proving to him that you are really listening and inter-ested. Parents can sometimes be token listeners. Count how many times you say "Yes, dear" each day. Did you really mean "yes" or did you send him the signal, "I don't really care what you said. As long as you stay off my back, any old response from me should do."?

Building on the child's statement is a great way to keep a "conversation" going, even when the child only says one word for every five the parent says.

IV: Talk to Yourself; We Won't Tell

You may have heard that it isn't dangerous to talk to yourself, but you ought to worry when you begin to answer. Pay no attention to such sentiments, because we are about to encourage you to talk to yourself, and to answer as well. Many times throughout the day, parents are engaged in activities in which their children are not directly involved, and yet the child is in the same room or nearby. It is tempting at such times to silently go about your business and capitalize upon the opportunity to get some things done. After all, immediate attention from your child is not being demanded.

These are excellent opportunities for meaningful language stimulation, however. What we are suggesting is that you keep a running conversation going, in simple sentences and phrases, describing what you are doing and what you are thinking. For example, if you are dusting the living room:

Parent: "The dust rag needs polish. Pour it on. Pour it on. What's first? The coffee table. Pretty table; I like it. First, I move the ash tray. Dust the top, dust the top. See it shine," etc.

Sounds a bit strange, you say . . . an adult talking to herself in short little sentences and phrases? Well, it may seem strange, but it serves some important language stimulation functions. Obviously, we don't expect this to be a 24–hour–a–day process. Remember, you are talking to yourself, not to your child. Don't expect him to respond or react.

Remember these simple rules:

Keep it simple and in short phrases.
Describe what you are seeing.
Describe what you are doing.
Describe what you are thinking.
Don't expect your child to respond directly.

V: Parallel Your Child's Silent Play With Verbal Description

Language develops first in the silent thought of a child's mind before it shows up in the speech we hear. For this reason, it is a good idea to help that process along by supplying language stimulation when no speech is heard. You will need to combine some guesswork with some tact in order to carry this off effectively. As your child plays nearby, you should supply him with short phrases describing what *he* is doing. For example:

"There's the cup. If I hit the cup on the floor it makes a noise. A big noise. Bang, bang, bang, bang. Cup. My cup. Bang the cup."

In part, you are naming objects that will expand vocabulary, but just as important, you are giving sentence form to the thoughts of your child. If you can guess correctly and can parallel his actions and thoughts, you are putting words and sentences in his mind for future reference.

Although this activity may sound a bit stilted and unnatural, you will find that it comes easily and may be something you are already doing. But don't get carried away! A little of this repeated several times a day goes a long way.

VI: Isolate Small Elements of Language To Build On

As language develops, children acquire rules that guide their speaking. The growth in rule–acquisition is rapid, natural, and continuous over a three– or four–year period.

When a child is having difficulty, however, something needs to be done to make the various language rules more visible and understandable. This does not mean that you should tell the child that all of these words are nouns or verbs, etc., but it would help if you emphasize one element at a time.

For example, you have determined that your child should learn that adding an /s/ or /z/ sound to the end of a word can mean that you are talking about more than one object (pluralizing nouns). All family members should have the "assignment" of pointing out to the child at least three things each day that are found alone, and also in groups of more than one. Setting the table may sound like this:

"One spoon for Bob, two spoons for Dad."
"One fork for Dad, two forks for you." (You may have to reset the table later, but you have made your point.)

It is best if you start with things the child can see, touch, move about, and play with, but the general idea is simple enough. Set your goals on some small aspect of language and give your child so many examples of that aspect that he will learn the distinction being made.

The above suggestions are general and could be applied to all language stimulation activities and at all levels of language learning. Now we will get specific and attempt to spell out activities that will be helpful for each of the various steps along the language–learning path. The clinician or professional who gave this book to you has identified those sections that will be of most benefit to your child.

The first task is to determine where your child is in his language-learning process. While expert testing and evaluation may be helpful, you too can determine the language level of your child. See the checklist at the end of this book (see Appendix B, page 93).

WORDS – THE BUILDING BLOCKS OF LANGUAGE LEARNING

Vocabulary development is an important part of every child's early learning. Throughout this book we are stressing the child's spoken language development, but it is important to remember that children have "understanding vocabularies" as well as "spoken" ones. That is, they understand words, and they speak words, and they *always* understand more than they speak.

Some children who don't speak any words at all can understand nearly everything that is spoken to them. Vocabulary learning, and language–learning in general, is an internal type of of activity that takes place in the brain. However, since we are concerned that your child uses his language to speak, we will emphasize speech and spoken language.

What is a word? Some parents report that their child spoke his first word when he was five months old. What that parent really heard was not a word as such, but sounds that the child made which happened to sound like a word in our language. Those sounds only become a word when the child uses them consistently to refer to a certain object, action, location, etc.

When an infant of five months lies in his crib saying, "Ma, ma, ma, ma," he isn't calling for his mother; he is vocally playing with sound for his own enjoyment and pleasure. Eventually the child will come to use the sounds in certain combination to refer to objects in his environment or to relate experiences. As he does, he is developing words in the true sense.

Strangely, we will accept a word as a word even if the sounds are not accurately produced. The fifteen–month–old may say "wawa" for water, and that is a perfectly good "word" since it relates to something in his environment.

In helping your child increase his spoken vocabulary, it is well to remind yourself that there is no direct relationship between the words and what they represent. There is nothing about the sounds of the word "chair" that make it refer to something we sit on. The word does not have any "chairness." This is obvious, but we remind you of it since we sometimes take for granted a child's learning of word meanings. Words have meanings because all of the people who use the language have agreed that certain sounds mean certain things. A young child has not yet learned this, however, and you will have to help him make the connection between words and what they mean.

There are several crucial elements in vocabulary learning:

1. The child does not learn a word as a meaningful sound until he has experienced it in a variety of ways. How many ways can a person "sense" an apple? He can look at it, touch it, taste it, smell it, hear it (if it's crisp). All these perceptions are necessary before the word can be learned. As you have seen, we recommend picture books for language assistance, but real objects are far better. It is important for the child to have as many experiences with the object as possible before he learns the name. Remember, understanding comes before speaking!

2. The word to be learned must be presented when the object (or experience) is present. Do everything you can to make clear the association between sound and what it refers to.

3. Repetition is crucial. Some children need ten repetitions of a word before they will attempt it, while others may need two hundred. A skilled parent can find fifteen different ways to say the word "shirt" while dressing his child. For example:
   Which shirt do you want to wear?
   How about this shirt?
   Shirt (holding up the shirt).
   Yellow shirt.

I like this shirt too.
Hands in the shirt.
Head in the shirt.
The shirt's on.

4. Hearing and seeing what the word is NOT is also important. The knowledge that a hat is a hat is, in part, related to the knowledge that anything else is not a hat. When you think of it, everything in the universe can fit into two categories: it is a hat, or it isn't a hat. It becomes important, then, to point out to your child things that are not what you are currently working toward. Parents generally do this in a kidding fashion, "Here's your hat" (handing the child a shoe). "This isn't a hat! Not a hat!" We generally find it best to start by pointing out what something is, and then what it is not. For example, it is better to say "This is not a hat," than to say "This is a hat, and this is a shoe."

5. Word use will develop in relation to meaningful situations in the home, and the best learning takes place when all possible circumstances are used. These various situations might include:

   a. circumstances where the child needs or wants something. When a child wants to play with his favorite truck, he may be more motivated to say "truck" than at another time. And if this truck is kept out of reach so the child needs to ask — all the better.

   b. circumstances where the object to be named is visible. If he sees his favorite toy car, he may be motivated to say the word.

   c. children say words they are told to say. The child says a word because his parents, or a sibling, have prompted him to do so. "Here comes dada; say dada."

   d. some words are spoken by children because the word fits perfectly into the sentence. Children are good pattern-learners and will attempt to "fill in the blanks" in others' conversations. We have heard children who will complete the statements of their parents, such as "Pass the salt and _____ . You are a big boy, soooo _____ . What do you put on your bread? Bread and _____ ."

   e. children eventually acquire words because words bring results. People *do* things when the words are spoken, and that is really what language is all about — getting people to do the things we want them to do. Some theorists have gone as far as to advocate "paying" the child for his language, but we feel that the best payoff is your natural and spontaneous response. If your child says "More ice cream, please," and gets more ice cream, he has learned that language works. It's magic! You must now set out to prove that words work, and this can be a most rewarding task. Remember, you are not seeking absolute clarity of speech at this point. If you are working to develop a speaking vocabulary in your child, accept and reinforce words that are close to the target. If he says "Sue" for "shoe" or "ba" for "ball," let him know that you understand. A good parental response in such cases would be "Yes, that's a shoe, shoe." You have then done two things: you've shown the child that he said a *word* (reinforce him) and you've given him the proper model of how the word is said. To say "No, say *shoe,*" will punish the word attempt and slow the process.

6. Many parents find scrapbooks helpful in building vocabularies, using pictures of the child himself, family members, or simply pictures from an old catalog. It is a good idea to set up a theme for each section of the book. For example, Section I could be entitled "This is me (or the child's name)," with individual pictures such as "My face," "My hand," "My ear," etc. Other possible subjects for pictures are the child's room and furniture, and other rooms in the house. This general idea can be expanded to match your child's current level of understanding. You can set up pages of pictures of things that fall into such categories as "people I know," "things we eat at breakfast," "things that smell good," "things I like," "things that are dirty," "things that fly," etc. The important thing is that the category fits the child's ability to understand.

IF YOUR CHILD SPEAKS NO WORDS

We will now consider a few suggestions for language development activities that incorporate our general guidelines. Although certain words are used as suggested starting points, please remember that the most logical words to start with are the words that have the greatest significance to your child. Think about his world and what he does throughout the day and select your own words as starting points. General clues to choosing a word would include:

1. Is the word meaningful to your child?
2. The word should probably be the name of something (at least the first few should be).
3. The word should be short and uncomplicated (the word "ball" would be better than the word "jack-in-the-box").
4. The object to be named should be available, and it should be something the child enjoys.

BEFORE WORDS APPEAR

Several things that parents do with their very young children (eighteen months and younger) play a very important part in language learning. They appear to set the groundwork for later learning. Although these ideas may not be appropriate for your child, some may be adapted. Here is a short description of some of these early language teaching strategies that appear to be a part of natural child/adult play.

1. Before children learn to understand the meanings of words, they learn to respond to changes in people's voices. Parents use a great deal of *vocal variety* when talking to their children, and these inflections really help the child.

2. Early in the word learning process, parents give their child many clues as to what they mean. *Gestures, facial expression, posture, pointing,* etc., are all used to "help" the child learn word meanings.

3. Parent–child *play rituals* help the child learn some of the hidden rules of communicating. Games like "hide and seek," "pat-a-cake," "How big is baby? Sooo big," etc., help the baby learn to watch the speaker's face, take turns in talking, and establish an interest in communicating.

4. Parents use an amazing amount of *repetition* while talking with children. Repetition by itself is good, but even better is the repetition parents use when they change a small portion of what is said. An example of this might help:

> Where is Daddy?
> Where's Daddy?
> Where is he?

In that short conversation, the parent has shown the child how to combine two words into what is called a contracted form (where's) and that the word "he" can be substituted for "Daddy," so it must mean the same thing (at least in this sentence).

5. Language learning really increases once the child realizes that the sounds people make with their mouths (talking) are made for a purpose — *to communicate* — and they *refer* to something. When someone says "Get your coat on," this isn't just a series of sounds strung together, but rather, those sounds were meant to get someone to do something, and they refer to a certain action and object.

One-Word Activities

We have selected the word "Mama" as a demonstration word.

Natural

a. Set a goal of fifty statements that include the word "Mama" to be spoken by each family member every day. You will find that to be quite a task. If you have four people in your family, plus the child, that would amount to 1,400 stimulations of the word "Mama" in a week.

b. Find five snapshots of Mama and tape them in five major doorways throughout the house. These pictures should be at eye level for your child. Now establish the rule that each time anyone in the family goes through that doorway, he must say the word "Mama." A little variety might help, so make it legal to put the word in two-word phrases.

   "My Mama. Good Mama. Nice Mama. Pretty Mama. Tommy's Mama. There's Mama," etc.

c. Do you have a musically inclined family? How about substituting the target word in some favorite songs. "Hello, Dolly" becomes "Hello, Mama," and "Old McDonald Had a Farm" becomes "Young Mama Had a Farm." If this doesn't come naturally, find other ways to use the word.

d. Setting the table is another way: as you place the plates around the table, make sure Mama's plate gets special attention. A sample of your monologue would be: "Plate here, plate here, plate here, MAMA'S PLATE HERE, plate here." Then, "Knife here, knife here, knife here, MAMA'S KNIFE HERE." etc. Notice that we don't have you name each person's plate as you go around the table. This is the week for emphasizing the word "Mama," and the best way to do that is to make it something special — make it stand out. Bombard the child with the word — you can't overdo it.

Similar exclamations about Mama could be used when sorting clothes, washing dishes, etc. If it's Mama's it's *special.*

How can you get your child to say the word? Asking him to say "Mama" is sometimes very natural and works, but with some children this simply shuts up the child.

How about plotting with the other members of the family to prove that saying "Mama" gets results? At the dinner table, you could use the target word as a "Simon Says" type of device. If the person doesn't use the word "Mama" when asking mother to pass something, she is to say "Sorry, I can't do that." The person should then repeat, "Mama, please pass the salt." You will know how far you can take such activities, but remember that you are trying to encourage use of the word without undue pressure.

Structured

a. We call this the "Great Scott, There's Mama" game, but you can come up with a better one than this. Go through one of your child's favorite books and tape a picture of Mama on several pages. Now sit down with your child to look through the book. When you come to the surprise pages, make a great hoopla over Mama. If you get no reaction, don't pay any attention to the second "planted" picture. Children can't resist, and in most cases your child will make some attempt to point out the picture to you. You may have to prompt a bit by saying "What do you mean?" or "I don't see anything."

b. Purchase or make a set of hand puppets representing each member of your family — dogs and cats, too! Play with the puppets, naming them after your family members, and do some "pretend" family activities with the puppets. After the puppets have clearly been identified, hide the Mama puppet somewhere in the room and play a bit of "Where's Mama?" A prize for the first person to find and say "Mama" might be fun. How about a carrot stick or an apple slice as the reward?

c. Sometimes the word "Mama" means more than just "That is my Mama." It means "That belongs to my Mama." Take advantage of that by playing a game of "Whose Is It?" You'll need several family members for this one.

Using familiar articles of clothing, favorite toys, kitchen objects, or whatever, see whether people can guess who owns the various objects. Have it prearranged so that when you come to Mama's favorite dress or pair of shoes, none of the people playing can guess the answer. If rewards work well in your house, how about some party prizes?

d. How about a game of "Who's under the Sheet?" Place the sheet over one of the players. Then have the other players come into the room (they've been waiting in another room) and guess who is under the sheet. Again, you will need to plot with the other players so that nobody knows who it is when Mama is under the sheet.

Activities like these are intended to get your child saying single words. The possibilities are endless, and the theme is to have fun while getting the speech process underway. Build a core of as many words as possible. Other common first words include the names of common animals (bow wow, kitty, cow, etc.), no, dada, all gone, up, etc. Many of the child's first words refer to a specific object or thing, while others refer to an idea or characteristic of something (big, good, happy), possession (my), location (here, there), action (run, hit, go), and others. It is a good idea to develop a core of words of a variety of kinds before starting on the two-word level. You will probably find that your child will start two-word statements on his own, but if he does not, there are ways to help him get going.

More One-Word Activities

Before going on to the two-word level, we would like to give some more suggestions for another word at the one-word level. We have chosen the word "up" for demonstration purposes.

Natural

a. Set a goal, such as twenty productions of the target word for each family member every day. The idea is to expose your child to the word as frequently as possible.

b. While putting the groceries away, it will be quite easy to show what "up" means. The cereal goes up (pointing to a higher shelf), while the canned goods do not. At first, you might totally isolate the word "up" without any other conversation. When things are put away, high up, make a "big deal" of it — by pointing, climbing up on chairs, reaching, etc. In other words, you are bombarding him with the word.

In a ten–minute grocery–putting–away period, he may hear the target word spoken fifteen times with no other conversation taking place.

c. If you live in a multi–level house, you are in luck. How many times do you go up and down the stairs in a given day? Enough to provide plenty of language stimulation if each step up is punctuated with the word. At the end of the day, when those steps are even steeper, how about laying it on thick? Each step is a real effort, and the word gets full play . . . u-u-u-u-p-p. You wouldn't be above crawling up the steps, would you? That might just add a bit of dramatics and interest to the whole learning process.

d. Do you have a pet dog or cat? Calling him to come "up" can provide plenty of language stimulation. Our dog's name is Puffy, and a conversation with her might go something like this:

> Come on *up,* Puffy, Up! Up, Puffy! Come on, you can do it. Up, Puffy (patting my lap). Good dog. Up. Up. (Now holding her and letting her down, lift her up again.) Up, up. Puffy's up."

e. Shopping trips to stores that have elevators or escalators should provide some good examples of "up." If you know of a glass elevator that goes up and down the outside of a building, it may be worthwhile to stop and watch for a while. There, your child could watch people going up, and maybe even get a ride up himself. Of course, driving home from that trip, you should take advantage of every opportunity when you have a hill to drive *up.* No reason why you couldn't talk to your car a bit . . . "Oh, oh, here comes a hill that we will have to go up. Come on, good car. You can do it. Up the hill, up the hill, up, up."

Prompting your child to say the word shouldn't be too difficult. If he wants to come up on your lap or be picked up, he may currently be telling you with gestures. After you have given him a week or so of concentrated stimulation with the word, maybe it is time to stop understanding what his hands are saying. Remember, accept anything close to the word, even if it is only the vowel, "uh."

Prompting your child to say the word in the following circumstances may prove fruitful: when he wants to get up from his nap, when he is telling you where to put the cereal boxes, when he wants to get up in his chair for a meal, and when he is trying to tell you that his hat is up on the shelf (but you just can't seem to find it, and he keeps saying "Up, up, up").

Structured

a. All sorts of games are possible with a helium balloon. Have your child hold the string, and you "hide your eyes." Then have him let the balloon rise or hold it down. You guess which it is and then check to see whether you are correct. Reverse roles and have him guess.

If you lack a balloon filled with helium, try a toy airplane tied to a string that has the other end draped over the top of a door. What a great way to show the child that his speech can change things. When says "Up," the plane goes up (if you pull the end of the string).

b. A "Jack–in–the–Box" type of game is good for use of the word. Use a large box or several chairs, back to back, to form a square. Crouch down inside and pop up when someone says the magic word. You may have to get some other family members to say "up" the first few times, but if you are able to pop up as a real "surprise," your child will soon want to see you "up" again.

c. If you have a slide in your yard, you might act as the policeman who only allows people to go up on the steps when they ask "Up, please" (for the bigger kids), or just plain "Up" (for others).

Two–Word Combinations

By two years of age, most children have begun to combine two words into phrases. This is a very important step in language, since it signals the beginning of grammar. Your child is now going to have to decide which word should come first. Such a decision is at the heart of language learning.

Many times children will use one word in combination with many others. Such combinations as *"My* shoes, *my* horsie, *my* cookie, *my* boat, *my* dollie, and *my* mama" all have a similar pattern. Other such words would be "big, pretty, red, all gone, more." You should try to begin with words your child has already spoken, but this may not be necessary.

The existence and nonexistence of things tend to fascinate children. A good starting place will be the phrase "all gone."

Natural

a. Mealtime is a good time to work on the "all gone _____" combination. There should be plenty of examples to stimulate the child, such as "all gone milk, all gone potatoes," etc.

b. When emptying the sink after washing the dishes, you might point out the soap suds as they go down the drain. Eventually you will get an opportunity to prompt "all gone soap."

c. If you live where there is snow in the winter, you can combine a little science study with your language learning. Bring in a small bit of snow on a plate and let it melt. Maybe you could separate it into ten or fifteen parts and get an "all gone snow" for each one of them. If you live where there is no snow or it is summertime, see whether you can find some frost in the freezer section of the refrigerator to use in the same manner.

d. Washing hands could bring an "all gone dirt" or two. (Incidentally, if you feel more comfortable reversing the order to "dirt all gone," that is all right, too.)

e. While dialing the telephone, you might point out the sound of the dial tone. Once you begin to dial, the tone will be "all gone buzz."

Structured

a. The game of "Light's Out!" begins in the living room with all of the lights turned on. It might even be a good idea to import some lamps from other rooms to increase the possibilities. If you have a pen flashlight, turn it on and "hide" it someplace in the room. Obviously, since there is so much light in the room now, you would not be able to see the pen flashlight, and it would stay "hidden." Now set out, you and your child, on a search for the lost flashlight. Go from lamp to lamp turning each off as you come to it. Emphasize the phrase "all gone light" as each is turned off. As the room gets darker and darker, the penlight will soon become visible. When all the lights are off except the flashlight, go to it and turn it off. After you have led your child through this activity several times, have him hide the flashlight and lead you around the room. "All gone light!" is expected after each light is turned off.

As you might have guessed by now, such an activity would work well if you are working on single words, too. Simply use the word "off." You may also use the phrase "light off," if you wish. Remember, it is important to develop many other ideas to prompt use of the word–group "off." How about "shoe off, sock off, water off, soap off," etc.?

b. Depending upon your child's eating habits, collect a few of his favorite snack foods such as a couple of candies, a cracker, an apple slice, a carrot stick, a small marshmallow, etc. Maybe it would be best to have two or three sets of these snacks and then set about making them "all gone." First you take one and eat it, exclaiming, "all gone candy." Then go to the next and so on until your child wants to get into the act (probably that will be right away).

c. Try a game of "Bubble, Bubble." A bottle of the liquid that children use to blow bubbles is good for lots of language stimulation ideas. Blow so that a couple of bubbles are in the air. Then pop one at a time, making sure that you underscore "all gone bubble" as each one breaks. A little theatrics wouldn't hurt — let one get close to the floor or sneak up on another. After you have done a few, get your child into the bubble–popping act. (Do this outside or over a bare floor — the liquid is quite sticky.)

d. If your child is small, and you are quick, simply find a small object that attracts particular attention from your child and play a little game of "Sleight of Hand." Hold the object in one hand and then quickly toss it into the other with a gleeful "all gone marble." He may catch you at it, but all the better. Have him try to trick you with a few "all gones" of his own.

e. If your child is small, and you are deliberately not so quick, here is another idea. Get a large, empty oatmeal box (cylindrical). Cut a small hole in the bottom of the box, just large enough so that a penny falls through. Now present this "magic trick": place the lid of the oatmeal box on the bottom of the box so that the hole is not too visible. Then, with much fanfare, show him that there is no hole in the box (better move quickly). While removing the lid of the box tell him that you are going to put a penny in the oatmeal box and "make it disappear." Put the penny in the box and put the lid over the top. Place your hand over the hole in the bottom and shake the box until the penny comes through the hole into your hand. Open up the box and place the lid back on the bottom and show him "all gone penny." Depending upon your child's age, he will sooner or later catch on. When he does, encourage him to show you the same trick. Or better yet, let him try it on someone else in the family.

More Two-Word Combinations

A child's world revolves around himself, and so a good selection for an early phrase would be some word of ownership, such as "My _____." This is a little more difficult to prompt because as soon as you say "my shoe," you are referring to your own shoe, and the child's response might be "your shoe." Once your child has the concept of possession and ownership, however, this problem fades.

Natural

a. Several situations are prime candidates for using the phrase "My _____ ." When dressing yourself, you could easily stimulate your child with five or ten phrases such as "my sock, my shoe, my pants, my shirt, my dress, my skirt," etc. Dressing your child is a good opportunity to prompt him with "Whose shoes?" If he responds with his own name, that is fine. "Tommy shoe" is a perfectly good response and indicates that your child isn't quite ready for the more complicated response. You might then change to the phrase "Daddy's shoe," etc., and wait until more maturation takes place.

b. While washing your face, you could make a real production out of it. "My forehead, my nose, my chin," etc.

c. Another situation that appears to lend itself to possession-type phrases is setting the table. Don't comment at anyone's place except your own. "*My* knife, *my* spoon, *my* plate," etc.

Structured

a. Get an old pillowcase and fill it with some of your child's favorite possessions, along with some items that are easily identifiable as yours. Pull out one item at a time with the phrase "My pen, my watch, my book," etc. After you have chosen a few of yours, pull out something of your child's and see what response you get.

b. Do you have a couple of old photographs you wouldn't mind cutting up? One picture of you and one of your child would be all that is needed, but a couple more would be even better. Cut each picture so that various body parts are isolated — head, body, arms, and legs would be enough pieces.

Place all of the pieces of the picture in front of you as if it were a puzzle. Finding a part of your picture, exclaim "My arm," and begin the process of putting your picture back together. See if your child can go along with you and put himself together, too.

c. Let's go fishing! In most hardware or novelty shops you should be able to purchase a small magnet. Now buy a box of paper clips, and you are all set to go fishing. First, place a paper clip on each of two pictures — one of yourself and one of your child. Place the two pictures on the floor. Then place the magnet on a string attached to a short stick. Now you can go fishing. If you catch your picture, you say "My picture," and you get to keep it. If you catch the other picture, you have to throw it back. Variations on this game are unlimited.

And More

Children may combine two words to describe someone (or something) doing something. Examples might include statements like "Daddy go," "Mommy sit," "Baby cry," etc. At this level, you will also hear two words to refer to actions and to the object of actions — for example, "Push wagon," "Pet kitty," "Pat pillow." Some simple words that modify things are also added by many children. These words are almost always used to talk about *changes* in things, or unexpected qualities, such as "dirty sock," "dark room," "ishy peas," and "hot cup."

Natural

Try to take advantage of those times when things around the child change in an unexpected way. If the dog falls asleep with all four feet in the air, she's a "silly dog," or if the jelly spills on the table, it's a "sticky table." How about wet shoes, slippery shoes, noisy boys, etc.? Your day will be filled with opportunities to say these two-word combinations as a model for your child. The following conversation between parent and child will show several ways to encourage your child to say the words following your model:

Parent (in response to dog barking): "Dog bark."
Child: No response
Parent: "What is the dog doing?"
Child: "Bark."
Parent: "That's right — dog bark!" "The noisy _____ ."
Child: "Dog bark."

Structured

Place four objects on a table in front of the child (e.g., banana slices, a ball, a glass of water, a toy car). Show and say what you can do with each object (e.g., "eat banana," "throw ball," "drink water," "push car."). After several models of each, ask the child what to do with each. If he is correct (in two words), he gets to do the activity.

IF YOU HAVE COME THIS FAR

If your child is now starting to link two words together to make small statements, you have come a long way. First, and most significantly, your child has recognized the links between sounds and their meanings. This is the most important step in speech and language development. Second, your child has begun to link words together to make mini-sentences. Most children will now begin to build on these skills to make more and more statements about the world around them. As your child's language becomes more and more adult-like, you should review these ten ideas to make sure that he is getting the stimulation he needs to continue his language growth.

1. Make sure your child moves about the house rather than sitting or staying in the same place too long. This may sound a bit strange to some parents, but there are children who will stay in one place for long periods of time.

2. Change things around from time to time. This may come as a shock to the parent who has to move the furniture, but a simple change such as moving a chair to a different part of the room can provide an opportunity for language learning.

3. Don't put everything out of reach. Parents often say "Oh, he's at the age where I have to put everything up." We would like to encourage you to find some things that can be left in reach since they may provide nuggets of gold for exploration and learning. We are not talking about tiny glass knick-knacks, but rather, larger and more substantial items that can be picked up, felt, looked at, tasted, explored!

4. Use the television and radio to your advantage. Some people claim that television and radio are not good for children. Certainly, too much of either would work to slow some children's speech and language development. However, if you select the shows and limit the viewing and listening time,

the stimulation can be very broad. The children's shows on educational television are very beneficial.

5. Capitalize on daily events that may otherwise go unnoticed. The mailman can be an interesting fellow. Enlist him in your campaign for language growth. Make mail delivery a big event by greeting the mailman and making sure that your child "gets the mail" and looks it over with you.

6. Bring in new friends for your child to play with. One of the most frequent complaints we hear from parents is that their child doesn't have any playmates in the neighborhood. With some effort, you will be able to find appropriate playmates for your child. Seek them out. A variety of children is important. Bring them to your house one or two at a time, and try to let them have a free hand at playing. You must remember that kids play in very different ways at various ages. It is just as meaningful for two one–year–olds to play individual activities side by side as it is for older children to play formal games together. Don't force the children to do what you think is best; they will find the most natural way to get along.

7. Capitalize on special events. Birthdays, of course, can be great for some hoopla. How about celebrating some other events just to add variety to your child's world? Holidays can be great sources for extra household decorations, special meals, and family parties. You can also "celebrate" getting a new tooth, a particular household plant blooming, the dog's birthday, the first robin in spring, the first snowfall in winter, a new word! Try to find two or three events to celebrate each month; you'll soon be in the swing of it.

8. Planning a trip or vacation? We would like to suggest a way to make the trip three times the fun. Every trip has three main parts to it, and they each have a special type of fun involved. First comes the planning. Get out the maps, talk over the route and what to pack, plan motel stops, and talk about what you plan to see and do. This is half the fun! The second part of any trip or vacation is the actual event itself. There are so many ways to build in stimulating activities that they are too numerous to mention. We will just remind you that part of your goal on that upcoming trip is to see to it that your child is exposed to new things to see, hear, feel, smell, taste, and talk about. The last part of the trip will be the memories that follow. "Remember when" conversations

should stimulate your child's recall of things that he would like to talk about, too. Pictures help, but if you don't have any, a drawing or a picture postcard picked up along the way should prove a good tool to jog the memory.

9. Children's records are very good sources of added language stimulation. Get a variety of them: some that tell a story, some that have rhythm songs, some that provide picture books to go along, and so on.

10. Parents often find it difficult to keep a variety of toys available for their children. Prices are high, and the possibilities are limitless, so let's see if we can come up with a few ideas for inexpensive ways to vary the playthings available:

   a. How about a sandbox inside? Yes, our reaction was the same when we first heard of it, but you may find that a small box of sand placed in the basement can provide hours of play.

   b. Want an even bigger mess than the indoor sandbox? Put some food coloring in several pans of water and allow your child to mix and stir in the sink. The combinations are endless, and the fun is, too.

   c. Do you make your own bread? If so, a handful of dough makes for wonderful squishing and mushing. Children delight in watching the dough squeeze through their fingers and in pulling it from hand to hand.

   d. Go out and pick up a couple dozen small rocks from around the yard. Now, with a paintbrush and some paints, you and your child can have great fun painting designs on the rocks.

   e. How about cutting off some milk cartons and starting your own indoor garden? Children are amazed and fascinated by growing things.

   f. Do you have too small an apartment for a pet? Gerbils take up little room, are a great source of fun and entertainment, and are relatively easy to care for and feed. One word of caution: they do tend to reproduce . . . and reproduce . . . and reproduce . . .

Most children will continue to develop good language and speech once they have started, and you may find that all that will be necessary is the careful use of some general ideas in this book. However, some children will need continued help, and the remainder of this book is designed to provide a few ideas to keep the language process growing. Remember, your child hasn't read the text and doesn't know how children are supposed to learn to talk. He will develop in his own pattern. Don't try to impose someone else's ideas on him about what to learn and how to learn it. Neither this book nor any language expert can tell you exactly what your child is ready for next. All we have done is suggest some general guidelines, and it is up to you to choose and select as your child is ready.

BEYOND TWO WORDS

When your child reaches this stage, you should be on the alert for several things. Is he growing and changing in his communication skills with new vocabulary, longer sentences, new ideas, etc? Is he using language for a variety of reasons (e.g., to describe things, request, tell, etc.)? Is communication important to him? Are you able to understand many of the words he is saying?

From this point on, language gets very complicated. We have selected only a few areas on which to work and have provided a general sequence of steps. You should recall, however, that your child has not read the books on the steps of learning to talk, and his learning sequence may not be like other children's. Use what you hear in your child's speech as the most important guide for moving to new levels.

I: Noun + Verb + Object

Short sentences that contain a subject, verb, and object may soon be present in your child's speech (e.g., "Dad throw ball," "Bill cook soup," "Puffy eat crackers," "Mommie open pop").

You may have noticed that we have presented some examples for you to follow that give short, incomplete sentences (no "ands," "ifs," or "buts"). Professionals differ as to how wise it is to present these short sentences to children rather than use short, but complete, statements. Is it better to say "Mommie sets table" or "Mommie is setting the table"? There is no correct answer, but in our opinion, a child who is learning language normally can learn from *hearing* short complete sentences (such as "Mommie is setting the table") even though he might *say* the same thing as "Mommie set table." However, children with significant language learning difficulties may benefit from *some* short sentences where the smaller words are left out. Certainly you would not want to present only these types of sentences, but some will help. Our thinking is that even though these children understand the more complicated sentences just as well as they do the shorter ones, the real goal in talking is better stimulated through the incomplete sentence. Some adults find it awkward to speak like this, and our best advice is to do what comes naturally for you. We will give you some samples with the smaller words left out; but if they just sound too strange for you, go ahead and use them in the more complete form.

Natural

a. Since this particular sentence type consists of what we could call nouns, verbs, and objects of the verb, almost any every-day activity could be used as a model (e.g., "Mosquito bites David," "Hammer hits nail," etc.). Having popcorn tonight? Try taking a small bowl and feeding people in the room one kernel at a time, using the sentence "_____ eats pop-corn." After feeding each person, give a second small bowl to the child and see if he will go around the room doing the same thing.

b. Any task can be broken down into short noun–verb–object sentences. For example, when baking a cake, try to say simple sentences in the hope that they will elicit the same kind of response from your child. You can say "Mommie grease pan. Now it's your turn. Bobby grease pan. You do it and help me. Mommie flour pan. Mommie break egg. Mom-mie bake cake. Mommie frost cake." Your child may respond, "Bobby eat cake."

Structured

a. Play ball! Soft sponge rubber balls can be a lot of fun. Play "catch" with your child, finding as many ways to get the ball to him as possible. You can roll the ball, or throw, push, carry, bounce, or kick it, etc. Ask the child how he wants you to get the ball to him, and when he responds be sure to encourage him to say a whole sentence. The conversation might sound like this:

Parent: Do you want the ball?
Child: Yes.
Parent: How should I get it to you?
Child: Bounce.
Parent: I bounce ball – tell me to do it.
Child: Bounce it.
Parent: I can't hear you.
Child: You bounce ball.

b. Easter egg hunts are good all year 'round. Hide ten of your child's favorite playthings around the house and then go on a "toy hunt." When the child finds an object, you can say "Tommy found truck," etc. Just before he finds each object, you might cover your eyes and ask him to tell you what he is doing.

II: Noun + Verb + Location

Another common type of three–word sentence includes information about a location for an object or person.

Natural

a. Putting things away (e.g., laundry or dishes) is a natural time for such statements as "socks go here," "pants go there," "forks fit here," etc.

b. Many families have a set place for people to sit at the dinner table. It might be a good idea to indicate each evening where people sit: "Bob sits here, Jane sits here, Dad sits here," etc. After several days of this routine, change people's places and have the child assign their place each night.

Structured

a. You will need to enlist the help of an older child who doesn't mind being a bit of a character for this game. With your helper going with you, go around the house giving crazy directions for activities in certain places. For example, "Todd cries here, Todd smiles there, Todd hops here, Todd growls there," etc. Then have the older child give Todd a set of instructions alone the second time.

III: Verb + Noun + Location

Three–word sentences in young children's speech also may sound like this: "Throw ball here!" This type of sentence tells about an action happening to an object and adds the location of the action.

Natural

a. Again, any activity where you are putting things away will serve to prompt sentences. Groceries can be put away with sentences like "Put milk here," "Put soup there," and "Put crackers (on) shelf." Show the child some of the items and have him direct you as to where they go.

b. When kids come in from outside in winter, they have plenty of wraps to put away. Having a special place for each item not only helps the functioning of the house, but it also gives you an opportunity to model such sentences as "Hang coat (in) closet," "Put mittens (on) shelf," and "Set boots (on) floor," etc.

Structured

a. Before your child gets up from his nap, move five or six of the common pieces of furniture from their usual place to a rather unexpected place. Put a lamp in the kitchen sink (don't plug it in), and a chair on top of a table, etc. When the child wakes up, he will no doubt make comment about the strange state of things. Ask him to tell you where things belong to elicit such sentences as "Put chair here" and "Put lamp here." If your child is anything like ours, he will not be too "with it" for a while following a nap, so give him some time before starting into this activity.

b. A puzzle with puzzle parts that are whole objects, such as animals, helps with this activity. Take the puzzle apart, saying "Take dog out," "Take cat out." Then put the puzzle together again, encouraging him to tell you where to put each animal: "Put dog here," "Put cat here."

IV: Pronoun + Adjective + Noun

Sentences should start appearing in your child's speech that give indication of possession and that use words to modify. You may hear "My big truck, my dirty shoe," etc.

Natural

a. Any activity that includes sorting out things that belong to various family members could be used. Since color words may not be in the child's vocabulary, you may wish to use other modifiers, such as big, little, dirty, nice, pretty, good, bad, etc. The child may know the words "my" and "your" but not be using words like "his," "her," "their," etc. When sorting clothes, you can say "My big shirt," "Dad's clean sock," "Your nice pants," etc. Encourage similar sentences from the child by taking turns pulling clothes from a basket or putting them in the washer or dryer.

b. Use many of the earlier activities and modify them for this objective. Rows of family boots, labeled "My little boots," "Your big boots," "My dirty boots," and so on, will work for this type of language.

Structured

a. Put a number of possessions from each family member (as well as pets) in a large bag. Have your child pull them out and deliver them to the proper person: "My nice doll," "Your pretty mirror," "His (the dog's) dirty bone," etc.

V: Noun + Verb + Preposition + Object

The words "in" and "on" are often added in sentences of children about this time. You will hear sentences like "Ken sat on top," "He goes in there," and "We played in basement."

Natural

a. Outdoor play activities, especially at a local park or playground with other children around, are a good chance for moving about and stimulating sentences with prepositions: "I go down slide," "He goes on swing," "Mary climbs on tire." Encourage the child to tell you about his and others' activities. "What's next?" or "What is Johnny doing?" will help.

b. Putting toys away at night is another language opportunity: "Bear goes in box," or "Book goes on shelf." Encourage the child by asking him to tell you where the toy goes.

c. Mailing a letter? Let him put them in one at a time if he says "Letters go in box."

Structured

a. Get a piggy bank or use a jar with a slit in the top. Try putting the penny in where it will not fit and ask the child "Is that where it goes?" See if you can get him to respond "Penny goes in jar," or "Penny goes in here."

VI: "What" Questions

Natural

a. The "What" question develops in many children and becomes a solid part of their conversations. "Whatsat" is heard hundreds of times a day in many households. Children often use this word but don't really intend to be asking a question; rather, they are just touching base with the people around them. Take every opportunity (within reasonable limits) to respond to these naturally occurring questions with brief answers that use words you know the child understands. When you know that the child knows the answer to his question, give an unexpected answer:

Child: "Whatsat" (child points to his shoes)
Parent: "Orange juice."
Child: "What?"
Parent: "Oh . . . your shoe."

Structured

a. Find as many containers as you can that might hold familiar and unfamiliar objects, such as gift boxes, plastic Easter eggs, or milk cartons. Find several small favorite toys that can be hidden in the containers and play a game of "What's that?" or "What's in that?" — or whatever reflects your child's current language level. In every fourth or fifth container, place an unexpected object, such as a grape, a hard-boiled egg, or a shoelace. The surprises should encourage added conversation and keep up interest in finding out what each contains.

ON FROM HERE

Beyond this point, your child will learn language by adding new words and making longer and longer sentences. The following is a grouping of some of the various elements of language your child will be learning.

Words that indicate possession:

my	his–her
mine	Bobby's (the child's name)
me	Mama's or Daddy's
your	

Words that indicate position or relationship of things:

in	on top
on	between
over	under
beside	

Words that indicate a quality of something:

nice	pretty
big, small, tiny, etc.	dirty
red, blue, etc.	friendly

Words that start questions:

who	why
what	is
where	when

Words that indicate the negative or negation:

no   not   none

Words that link and indicate more than one:

and   but   or

The lists could go on and on. Obviously, each grouping of words does not simply represent a few isolated words to be learned as individual units, but rather groupings that all stand for a certain idea. The important thing the child learns is the ideas that the words stand for — to link other words, to indicate attributes of things, to show negative ideas, to ask a question, etc. This language–learning is a complicated business!

Since the lists could each become much larger, and the number of groups could be expanded greatly, we feel that it is impractical to attempt to continue outlining suggestions for each language stage. Instead, we will restate the basic idea that we used throughout the earlier work: the most important element of your work will be to *isolate a single "portion" of language for your child, emphasize it in your speech, bombard your child with examples, and encourage its use by your child.*

In order to know exactly which aspect to work on at any one given time, it may be best to listen to your child's speech and see what he is attempting to master. Maybe he is aware of plural concepts, so your task is to point out all of the examples you can find of one, and more than one, showing just how you make the word change to indicate the concept. You will recognize that rules of language are not very reliable. "Book" becomes "books," "sheet" becomes "sheets," "cap" becomes "caps," etc., but "child" doesn't become "childs" and "sheep" doesn't become "sheeps." Similarly, we change the tense of a verb in some strange ways: "walk" becomes "walked," "look" becomes "looked," "cook" becomes "cooked," etc., but "sing" doesn't become "singed," and "fly" doesn't become "flyed."

Most children are capable of learning this complicated system called speech and language with little or no special instruction. For the child who needs more, it can be a demanding yet rewarding experience for his family and teacher. Many qualities are necessary for the parents of children with language difficulties, but the most outstanding is determination. If this book provides you with the framework and motivation to stimulate you to continue trying, we feel our effort is worthwhile.

APPENDIX A

Activity Checklist

Section	Page	Read	Carry Out	Target Date
TO THE PARENTS				
Introduction				
The Target of this Book				
Danger Signals				
Some General Suggestions				
Special Recommendations				
PART I: Language–Related Skills				
Self-Awareness				
Body Image				
Self–Concept				
Motor Skill and Coordination				
Balance				
Locomotion				
Rhythm				
Eye-Hand Coordination				
PART II: Pre–Language Sensory Skills				
Visual				
Color — Discriminating Same or Different				
Color — Sorting and Grouping				
Color — Sequencing and Recall				
Shape — Discriminating Same or Different				
Shape — Sorting and Grouping				
Shape — Sequencing and Recall				
Size — Discriminating Same and Different				

Section	Page	Read	Carry Out	Target Date
Size — Sorting and Grouping				
Size — Sequencing and Recall				
Distance — Discriminating Same and Different				
Distance — Grouping and Sorting				
Distance — Sequencing and Recall				
Auditory				
Awareness of Sound				
Awareness of the Cause-Effect Relationship of Sound				
Identification of Sound				
Gross Sounds — Discrimination				
Gross Sounds — Sequencing and Recall				
Characteristics of Sounds				
Tactile				
Touch and Muscle Sense				
PART III: Language Development				
General Suggestions				
I: Model the Correct Language Target				
II: Expand Your Child's Statements Into More Complex Ones				
III: Keep the Thought Process Going With a Side Comment on the Child's Statement				
IV: Talk to Yourself: We Won't Tell				
V: Parallel Your Child's Silent Play With Verbal Description				
IV: Isolate Small Elements of Language To Build On				
Words — The Building Blocks of Language Learning				

Section	Page	Read	Carry Out	Target Date
If Your Child Speaks No Words				
Before Words Appear				
One-Word Activities				
More One-Word Activities				
Two-Word Combinations				
More Two-Word Combinations				
And More				
If You Have Come This Far				
Beyond Two Words				
I: Noun + Verb + Object				
II: Noun + Verb + Location				
III: Verb + Noun + Location				
IV: Pronoun + Adjective + Noun				
V: Noun + Verb + Preposition + Object				
VI: "What" Questions				
On From Here				

Questions about activities or child's responses (e.g., what worked, what did not work, what I changed).

Date for next conference: _____

Checklist of Your Child's Current Status

The following checklist may help you collect information about your child that could assist your language clinician. Look over the following material and then carefully observe your child over a two-week period. Try to answer as many of the items as you can each evening.

Check your reaction to each of the following:

	No Problem	May be a Problem	Definitely a Problem
stays interested in what is going on (attention span)	_____	_____	_____
is interested in people	_____	_____	_____
cooperates	_____	_____	_____
looks at people who are talking to him	_____	_____	_____
follows moving objects with his eyes	_____	_____	_____
looks at objects being talked about	_____	_____	_____
listens when people talk to him	_____	_____	_____
can imitate body movements (hop, jump, etc.)	_____	_____	_____
can imitate speech	_____	_____	_____
sounds	_____	_____	_____
words	_____	_____	_____
sentences	_____	_____	_____
understands when his name is called	_____	_____	_____
understands names of common household objects	_____	_____	_____
understands the word "no"	_____	_____	_____
understands the names of his body parts (head, feet, etc.)	_____	_____	_____
is interested in pre-communication rituals ("so-big," "peek-a-boo," "all gone")	_____	_____	_____
has a knowledge of same/different	_____	_____	_____
has a knowledge of matching/sorting	_____	_____	_____

	No Problem	May be a Problem	Definitely a Problem
is communication important to your child:			
with other children	_____	_____	_____
with adults	_____	_____	_____
for what purposes:			
to get things ("I want")	_____	_____	_____
to get people to do what he wants ("Don't do that.")	_____	_____	_____
to give information ("That's a shoe.")	_____	_____	_____
to be social ("Hi.")	_____	_____	_____
to describe an ongoing event ("The baby is crying.")	_____	_____	_____
to express her own personality ("I'm a big girl.")	_____	_____	_____
to get information ("Why?")	_____	_____	_____
to pretend ("I'm a big airplane.")	_____	_____	_____
to solve problems ("If I put it there, this part will fall.")	_____	_____	_____
to entertain ("Watch me while I dance for you.")	_____	_____	_____
does the child understand and respond appropriately to:			
directions	_____	_____	_____
questions	_____	_____	_____
requests	_____	_____	_____
commands	_____	_____	_____
similarities and differences	_____	_____	_____
statements of cause	_____	_____	_____
implications of actions	_____	_____	_____
predictions of outcome of events	_____	_____	_____
humor	_____	_____	_____
emotional tone of others	_____	_____	_____
gestures and body language	_____	_____	_____
common nouns	_____	_____	_____

	No Problem	May be a Problem	Definitely a Problem
verbs	_____	_____	_____
verb tense	_____	_____	_____
prepositions (in, on, over, beside, etc.)	_____	_____	_____
pronouns (I, me, you, we, he, she, him, etc.)	_____	_____	_____
adjectives (words that describe)	_____	_____	_____
plurals	_____	_____	_____
possession	_____	_____	_____
long complex sentences	_____	_____	_____

does the child use language to do any of the following:

	No Problem	May be a Problem	Definitely a Problem
name things	_____	_____	_____
indicate when more of something appears	_____	_____	_____
indicate disappearance of something	_____	_____	_____
indicate when something is gone	_____	_____	_____
indicate when an activity stops	_____	_____	_____
indicate possession	_____	_____	_____
indicate rejection of an idea	_____	_____	_____
indicate action	_____	_____	_____
indicate location	_____	_____	_____

does the child's speech contain:

	No Problem	May be a Problem	Definitely a Problem
negative sentences	_____	_____	_____
yes/no questions	_____	_____	_____
"Wh" questions (why, what, where, who)	_____	_____	_____
conjunctions	_____	_____	_____
pronouns	_____	_____	_____
possession	_____	_____	_____
plurals	_____	_____	_____
tense	_____	_____	_____

	No Problem	May be a Problem	Definitely a Problem
adjectives using "er" or "est"	_____	_____	_____
articles (a, an, the)	_____	_____	_____

How understandable is the child's speech (Circle one):

    easily intelligible   occasional words and phrases not intelligible

    intelligible if listener knows topic

    occasional words and phrases intelligible   completely unintelligible

How many total words does your child speak? _____

What is the longest sentence your child has spoken? _____

Does your child show understanding or use of the following? Circle those observed:

Space:	top, through, away from, next to, inside, in front, under, between, nearest, corner, behind, beside, center, side, below, right, forward, above, separated, in order, on, off, in, out, high low
Quantity:	some, not many, few, most, least, whole, half, as many, medium-sized, zero, every, pair, equal
Time:	between, first, second, third, last, near, after, never, always, soon, yesterday, tomorrow, morning, noon, afternoon, night, winter, spring, summer, fall
Color:	red, blue, green, yellow, orange, white, black
Shape:	round, square, triangle, circle, box, line, dot, tall, short
Texture:	smooth, rough, course, fine, soft, hard